Under the Spell of MOTHER EARTH

BERIT KJOS

Grace Thomson 3

VICTOR BOOKS®

A DIVISION OF SCRIPTURE PRESS PUBLICATIONS INC.
USA CANADA ENGLAND

Other Victor Books by Berit Kjos

A Wardrobe from the King
Under the Spell of Mother Earth

Scripture quotations are from the *Holy Bible, New International Version,* © 1973, 1978, 1984, International Bible Society. Used by permission of Zondervan Bible Publishers. Other quotations are from the *New American Standard Bible,* © the Lockman Foundation (NASB) 1960, 1962, 1963, 1968, 1971, 1972, 1973, 1975, 1977.

Copyediting: Carole Streeter and Barbara Williams
Cover Design: Paul Higdon
Cover Photo: The Image Bank

Library of Congress Cataloging-in-Publication Data

Kjos, Berit.
    Under the spell of Mother Earth / by Berit Kjos.
        p.   cm.
    Includes bibliographical references (p.   ) and index.
    ISBN 0-89693-850-6
    1. New Age movement. 2. Nature worship. I. Title
BP605.N48K56 1992
261.2—dc20
                                                              91-34575
                                                               CIP

---

2 3 4 5 6 7 8 9 10 Printing/Year 96 95 94 93 92

CONTENTS

"With paganism on the rise and the Earth Goddess beckoning, Berit Kjos' Christian critique of this misguided spirituality is timely and on target."

Doug Groothuis author of *Unmasking the New Age*, *Confronting the New Age*, and *Revealing the New Age Jesus*.

Foreword

I GAVE BERIT KJOS a big affirming hug last spring when she told me about the book she was writing, little realizing it would be a book that every parent should read.

Here is a shocking revelation of the master plan of Satan for a resurgence in America of the pagan religions of Babylonian days. A spiritual renaissance is sweeping our nation—but it is not from God. Good environmental practices are mixing with the false philosophy of "The Earth is our Mother," even worshiping her. Witchcraft is masquerading as environmental spirituality.

The author documents school classrooms' hypnotic exercises of oneness with the earth, the practicing of witchcraft, Hatha yoga, native American spiritism, and students having spirit guides. She shows how myths of gods and goddesses are replacing factual knowledge.

The best-read books in schools and libraries are scary, mystical stories that blur reality with fantasy. Science fiction in science courses destroys students' rational thinking, and cartoons beckon children to experience magical forces and witchcraft's mind control.

But Berit doesn't just define this horrifying problem. Her "What Can Families Do?" sections teach how to pray and prepare our children for this spiritual deception by discussing listed key truths with our families, sending us directly to the Bible for God's answers.

The book encourages Christians to prayerfully consider how we have misused the environment. The list of family projects to save the environment God's way are extremely helpful.

Berit rightly teaches that people are more important than

the environment. How to have a personal relationship with Jesus along with steps to wholeness in Him, not Mother Earth or evil spiritual beings, makes this an extremely victorious—and practical—book.

This book is must reading for all parents, Christian education workers, school teachers, and superintendents of schools.

Evelyn Christenson
February 1992

A Parable

AT FIRST NO one noticed him. Hidden by the night, the Maker wandered silently through the pathless virgin forest. Yet nothing was hidden to him. He had planned and written every detail of nature in his mind an eternity ago. Now—after immeasurable waiting and longing—He was finally walking in his woods, smelling the scent of cedars, feeling dew-wet moss under His feet, watching a sparrow sleep in its nest. . . . The darkness, like the coming day, throbbed with life and promise.

As the light of dawn spread across the horizon, the Maker reached a clearing overlooking the valley. What a view! Distant hills sparkled with waterfalls and dancing fountains. Crystal-clear streams leapt downward over rocks and moss until they all flowed together, forming a river which shimmered with the golden glow of the rising sun. It wound its way through lush meadows filled with fragrant fruit trees, grapevines, berries, and blossoms in a breathtaking display of love's creativity.

"Beautiful!" As He whispered the word, unspeakable joy welled up inside Him. Flinging out His arms, He sang out to the world, and every rock and ridge echoed back: "It is perfect!"

Awakened, a choir of birds burst into song, and others— crickets, bees, oxen, and lions—joined together in a symphony of sounds. The Maker laughed. A doe lifted her head and looked into His kind, happy face with adoring eyes. A cougar jumped down from a tree and laid its head near His feet. Unafraid, a small flock of sheep ran to meet Him.

The Maker bent down, picked up a lamb and cradled it in His arms. "Dear little one," He whispered tenderly, "if only

My people would always trust Me as you do this moment. Then the splendor would last." He returned the lamb to its mother and walked toward the river.

Near the bank, a man and woman were picking berries and feeding them to the animals that gathered around them. The Maker stopped to watch. "Harmony reigns today," He mused, "but its enemy plots war against My children's innocence, against My plans, against Me...." The glimpse of future pain brought a stab of sorrow. He knew the time had come to share His heart with His precious human companions—and to show them how to preserve this beauty. But would they understand His plan, respond to His love, and cherish the relationship He offered them? Would the challenges ahead cause them to turn to Him for wisdom and strength? Or would they seek counterfeit power and become enslaved? The answers tore at His heart.

"Don't forget, dear children," He whispered. But tears welled up in His eyes, for He saw their weakness.

The Destroyer spoke first to the woman. He looked charming in his shiny garments, and his voice sounded smooth as silk. "Don't worry about those instructions. The Maker wouldn't deny you His best gifts, would He?"

"But didn't He say? ..."

"The details aren't that important. Just remember that He wants you to be happy. Follow your feelings. Your own desires will lead to life, not death. You'll find hidden wisdom—wisdom to become a maker yourself...."

"Really?" It seemed so good.

The woman believed and convinced the man.

Generations passed. No longer innocent, people everywhere listened to the seductive voice of the shining one. Few remembered the Maker.

"Let the stars guide you," coaxed the Destroyer. "Tune your minds to the spirits of trees and rocks. Draw strength from the mountain, the eagle, the oak, the goddess.... Use drums, drugs, chants, and sex. Ecstatic rites will connect your minds to Mother Earth and invoke her forces."

Fascinated by the false promises, the people followed.

"Build a tower reaching to heaven," the voice continued, "so all can be as one. Worship the god of the sun and the goddess of moons. They will empower you to remake the world."

Brokenhearted, the Maker watched. "My children were born free," He whispered, "yet they have become slaves to evil—to a mythical distortion of the good I offered them."

His thoughts carried Him to the end of time, when He would permit the Destroyer to fulfill His global plan—for a moment. "But this is too soon," He said to Himself.

At the Maker's command, the illusion of oneness was broken and the people scattered.

Ages passed. Nations pursued the visions of the shining one, but found neither peace nor fulfillment. Apart from the Maker's calming touch, nature turned cruel. Rains ceased. Rivers dried. Droughts brought famine, disease, and war. Longing to comfort and provide, the Maker sent messengers to bring the broken and lost back to His care.

Some believed and came. When they followed His guidelines, the rivers flowed with clean water and the land bore grain in abundance. But apathy and waste usually followed health and wealth.

"Let the weak follow the Maker," the proud would boast. "We can take care of ourselves!"

Barely visible in the cloudy moonlight, shadowy figures were moving toward an open field. Standing on a large, flat rock near the center, the Destroyer surveyed his gathering armies. "Hurry!" he screamed in a voice opposite the one he used to lure humans. "We don't have all night. The twentieth century has almost passed."

The dark forms were still scurrying to their places, when the Destroyer began his interrogation.

"Three waves of deception were planned for this generation. Two have passed. What happened? Where are we now?"

"The first wave, the youth rebellion, went well, sir," reported a trembling captain. "We appealed to their noble but naive idealism, emphasized the hypocrisy of their elders, and suggested they remake the world according to your wisdom, sir."

"Ah, good. How did they respond?"

"They loved your ancient practices, sir. Free sex, entrancing rituals along with drugs, drums, and meditation to alter consciousness and make spiritual connections. . . . Everything we suggested fit their own desires."

"Fine, fine. How are those fools serving us, now?"

"That brings us to the second wave, sir. Determined to spread your wisdom, many became your most faithful teachers, artists, entertainers, politicians, and media messengers. They taught and demonstrated your ancient ways until many of your practices became quite acceptable to the masses."

"What about the resistance—and the Maker's disgusting manual?" The icy chill in the Destroyer's voice sent a shiver through his armies.

"Banned!" shouted a bold ruler. "His guidelines are no longer permitted in public places—and the media ignores them. Of course, *your* religions are filling the gap."

Looking up at the full moon, the Destroyer grimaced. "We are ready . . ." he paused a moment, "for the third wave." Suddenly he began to laugh—a cold, hateful cackle which turned his cruel face purple. The watching armies cringed with anxiety.

"The third wave!" he repeated when he caught his breath. "Back to nature and its—I mean—our—secret wisdom! Ecological spirituality. Earth-centered environmental religion. All is one. The notion that nature is its own divine maker."

"What do you mean, sir?" asked the captain.

"Look around you," hissed the Destroyer. "See the pollution, waste, famine, death. . . ."

"Yes, I had this great idea," boasted a commander. "I urge people to litter and waste. 'Just toss it,' I whisper into their minds. . . ."

"That was *my* idea, not yours!" screamed the Destroyer. "*I've always* told people to pollute. Pollution and destruction fit my plan."

The impulsive officer slunk away as Destroyer continued.

"The simplest way to spoil the earth is to lure people away from the despicable Maker. When they forget Him and His vile manual, the earth suffers. Then we can blame Him for the destruction, and convince people that *my* way—my natural kind of oneness—will heal the earth."

"Why should they believe us?" bellowed a loud voice from the mass of soldiers. "The nations you already control are in far worse condition than these lands."

"No problem, you lunkhead," yelled the ruler. "We've already weaned the people away from facts. Now they want myths to live by just as in the old days. Our writers have introduced a delightful assortment of old and new stories. Our loyal artists are painting images that will make them come alive.

"Children are learning to hear the wisdom of Mother Earth. I order my slaves to masquerade as tree spirits, river gods, love goddesses, whichever voice those fools want to hear."

"Good work," purred the Destroyer. "Be those voices. And what will they say?"

"That humans can help restore nature's original harmony if only they will believe in Self, connect with the Earth, and follow the spirits of nature."

The Maker watched from a nearby hillside. A white-clad messenger arrived, bowed, and knelt silently before Him.

The Maker touched his shoulders. "I understand your grief," He said softly. "My people suffer much pain and confusion. Continue to guard and encourage them. Remind them that they are on the winning side. Even the worst of the Destroyer's schemes will ultimately serve our purpose."

"Yes, my King." The angel looked up into the gentle face of the Maker. "The struggle is intensifying, but it has awakened Your people."

Another angel arrived. "I bring good news," he announced. "There's an army of people out there who worship only You. Some continue to spread Your love in schools. Others broadcast Your warnings and demonstrate *Your* power to heal wounded soldiers and restore damaged lands. Though many feel weary and isolated, Your people are rising together against the false unity of the Destroyer."

The Maker glanced at the dark armies below. "Those poor rebels fight a losing battle—and they know it, in spite of their bravado." A quiet joy filled His voice as He continued. "The powers of heaven belong to Me, and the earth is in My hands. Nothing can defeat those who love Me and share My concerns. Watch and see the final victory."

ONE

Is Earth
Our Mother?

To mark Earth Day, four women and two men stood on a hilltop outside Mount Horeb, Wisconsin, literally praying to Mother Earth. "Sacred Earth Power, bring healing to Planet Earth," intoned barefoot Selena Fox, priestess of Circle Sanctuary.... Similar nature worship was part of Earth Day festivals from Boston...to Berkeley.... The ceremonies were part of a growing U.S. spiritual movement: Goddess worship, the effort to create a female-centered focus for spiritual expression.
—Richard Ostling, *Time*, May 1991[1]

In the late twentieth century there is a growing awareness that we are doomed as a species and planet unless we have a radical change of consciousness. The reemergence of the Goddess is becoming the symbol and metaphor for this transformation...[and] has led to a new earth-based spirituality.
—Elinor Gadon, *The Once and Future Goddess*[2]

This is what God the Lord says—He who created the heavens and stretched them out, who spread out the earth and all that comes out of it...I Am the Lord; That is My name! I will not give My glory to another. (Isaiah 42:5, 8)

As a child, I loved to explore the Norwegian woods, fjords, and mountains with my father. He wanted me to fully enjoy all the wonders of nature; therefore, he would always point out the dangers as well as the delights. Before I could gather my favorite mushrooms, my father showed me how to spot poisonous ones. Before I could ski across the mountain wilderness, he taught me basic survival skills. My favorite reward was reaching the top, relishing the view, and eating the chocolates he always carried in his backpack. Heaven forbid that I should leave the wrappers behind, or fail to pick up another person's litter.

Eager to care for God's creatures, my friends and I turned our garage into a neighborhood animal hospital. Birds with broken wings, battle-torn cats, mangled mice, and abandoned litters of newborn kittens filled towel-lined boxes along the wall. We tried to give the best emergency care possible, but our knowledge extended no further than our own personal experience. Consequently, we poured brown iodine on every sore, dripped milk down semiconscious throats, and tried to stabilize broken limbs and wings with homemade splints. Perhaps our greatest mission was to offer each animal a loving, if not comfortable, place to die— and a spot in our backyard cemetery.

I wanted to be part of God's team of earth stewards who helped take care of His creation. I still do. But finding like-minded team members in our fast-changing culture has become complicated. The beliefs and practices associated with ecology stray far beyond biblical bounds—even in the church.

My first exposure to unbiblical environmentalism under the banner of Christianity came in 1990. I had driven to a mainline church some distance from my home to see how God's people would celebrate Earth Day. Watching the worship, I wondered if the Creator Himself would have been welcome. At one point, the members of the youth group stepped forward to present *their* offerings:

"I bring to our Mother, the Earth, the gift of a new beginning . . ."

"I bring to our Mother, the Earth, the birth of a new consciousness."

"I bring to our Mother, the Earth, the gift of immortality that you may live forever cherished by your beloved children."

The congregation responded to this strange ritual with a standing ovation. Did these people know whom they worshiped? Had environmental concern swung church doors wide open to paganism? Could this really be happening in a supposedly conservative church?

Earlier in the program, a young woman minister had danced her interpretation of the Creation story. Throughout the graceful performance, a voice narrated the creative acts of a female deity referred to as "she" or "her." At one point, "she" gave birth to earthly life—here the dancer crouched on stage and birthed an inflated globe.

Nature worship in the church? A Mother Goddess in place of God our Father? Grieved, I thought about the spreading delusion prophesied in 2 Thessalonians 2, when lawlessness would soar and blinded followers of counterfeit wonders would "perish because they *refuse to love truth*," when people would reject sound doctrine and follow teachers who tickle their ears (2 *Timothy* 4:3-4). Could we have reached that time?

Donald Bloesch, theology professor at Dubuque Theological Seminary seems to think so. His article in *Christianity Today*, "Lost in Mystical Myths," describes the spiritual renaissance that is sweeping through churches and seminaries, bringing pagan empowerment rituals and texts such as *Mother Earth Spirituality:* "The new spirituality represents a kind of naturalistic mysticism, a reemergence of the ancient religion of the Earth Mother."[3] This unholy renewal lures children as well as adults, atheists as well as Christians. No part of our culture is immune. Look at the signs of change in our schools and media.

Religion Returns to the Classroom.
The ban on religion in public schools failed to block the promotion of pagan beliefs. Spiritual buzzwords like *reverence*—suggesting a response reserved for the Creator Himself, and *connectedness*—referring to pantheistic oneness rather than biological interdependence, flow through environmental teaching and songs, persuading our children to love Mother Earth instead of God our Father.

During Earth Day 1990 celebrations, children wrote poems to Our Mother, visualized her healing, used guided imagery to connect with her spirits, and committed their lives to her preservation. Students in Brainerd, Minnesota watched a video titled *Spaceship Earth: Our Global Environment*, the ecological portion of a global education program.

A medley of Mother Earth's ambassadors shared their beliefs:

> *Noel Brown, Director, United Nations Environmental Program:* We need to develop a better sense of connectedness with all of life and when that reverence is developed, I think we'll find ourselves more at home and at ease in this world.

> *Sting, international rock singer:* The Indians believe that the spirits live in the trees, that the spirits live in the river, that the spirit is in the air. I think we used to believe that in the past ... and ... if there's a spirit in a tree, you don't just chop it down and burn it.

> *Girl:* I can't separate the destruction of the earth from the destruction of myself.... Because we all started out from the earth, we're all going to go back to the earth. The Native Americans called it Mother Earth, and it is.

> *Picture of Mother Earth wearing a gas mask:* This is your Mother speaking—I gave you life.[4]

In the same Minnesota classroom, one fifth-grader withstood the pressure to conform. In addition to the above video, his teacher celebrated Earth Day by infusing an old Gospel song with a contemporary message: *"We've* Got the Whole Earth in *Our* Hands!" Josh, who knew God as the Maker and Keeper of His creation, recognized the lie and refused to sing.

The Media and Mother Earth.

Reaching far beyond schools and churches, television beams environmental spirituality right into our homes. Perhaps you watched Hollywood's star-studded Earth Day 1990 dramatization of a dying Mother Earth. You may have welcomed her practical suggestions: *recycle, reuse, reduce* consumption and return to simpler living. Did you also notice a more subtle message? Wrapped in noble sentiments, it taught the basics of ancient earth-based religions: The earth lives, thinks, is our Mother, gave us life, deserves our worship.

"But," you might ask, "people have called earth our Mother for centuries. What is wrong with that?"

Not much—some years ago. But today's cultural climate differs. A generation ago, we viewed myths about Mother Earth as interesting fables from the past. But our time-tested filters for reality—biblical *truth* and scientific *facts*—are being replaced by wishful speculation and personal opinions. Today, anything is believable—true or not—if it *feels* right and supports your views.

This atmosphere breeds irrational and imaginary solutions. So when environmental leaders promote pagan nature religions as a means to connect with the earth and hear "her wisdom," people believe them. When public schools, popular books, and the media spread this alluring message, it soon takes root in the social mind-set.

And what is that message? To save the earth, explains nature theologian Thomas Berry, "a new descent into a more primitive state must then come about."[5] His influential book, *The Dream of the Earth*, the first volume in the Sierra Club's series on nature and philosophy, explains how "a new type of religious orientation . . . must emerge from our *new story* of the universe." (emphasis added)[6]

Cable king Ted Turner has provided just such a "new story." His cartoon series, *Captain Planet*, exemplifies the spiritual message that permeates environmental teaching. It beckons children to connect with magical forces, exercises the mind control formulas taught by contemporary witches, learns from benevolent shamans (pagan priests and healers), and trusts the wisdom of goddess Gaia, mother of all life.

It also illustrates the vision of Turner's Better World Society: environmental consciousness with his own formula for social reform. By raising public awareness, presenting a new view of reality, and rewriting the Ten Commandments—"I promise to have love and respect for Planet Earth . . . "[7] instead of "I am the Lord your God. You shall have no other gods before Me"—he hopes to build a world of peace and oneness—*without God*.

Viewers of *Captain Planet* were told to protect the earth and fight exploitation using Gaia Power. Notice the seductive blend of environmental wisdom, cultural bias, and pagan spiritism in Episode One:

The earth shakes as Hoggish Greedly's huge earthmover lumbers through the forest, uprooting trees and awakening beautiful goddess Gaia.

"My goodness, can't the spirit of the earth take a little nap? What's going on?" She touches a crystal dome which, like a diviner's crystal ball, fills with the image of Greedly's oil rig.

"Ah. It's those poor, silly humans again. They're going to destroy my planet if they keep going like this. What's a mother to do?" Scanning the earth through the crystal, she sees polluted rivers, ugly smokestacks, and barren stumps of clear-cut mountain sides.

She gasps and activates her emergency plan: the planeteers. She chooses five children from around the world, empowers them with magic rings that control *earth, water, wind,* and *fire,* then sends them out to battle evil Greedly. On the way, the fifth planeteer exercises his power, *psychic telepathy,* to invoke Gaia's spiritual presence. The image of the Goddess speaks: "You must have faith in yourselves, planeteers, because you're fighting for the good of the whole world."

Moments later, when Greedly threatens to spray oil on coastal wildlife, the five children *form* a circle, *focus* their minds, *speak* their magic words, and *project* their powers—a standard withcraft ritual. Captain Planet materializes in their midst and explains, "I am your powers combined and magnified!"

In the final glow of victory, the valiant superhero invites his viewers to join the crusade on behalf of the earth. His parting promise sounds almost irresistible: *"THE POWER IS YOURS!"*

The power is whose?

One of the lures of pagan religions is the belief that nature's power can be harnessed by humans. That was Satan's bait from the beginning: "You will be like God!" With a few magic formulas, all seekers can learn to manipulate the force.

But can they? Those who try eventually discover that the occult force controls them—with devastating consequences. The Apostle John explains why: "The whole world is under the control of the evil one." Then he points us to the only way to genuine peace and harmony: "The Son of God has come and has given us understanding, so that we may know Him who is true" *(1 John 5:19-20)*.

How do we respond to mixed messages such as Turner's? Do we join his crusade but reject his power source? Or do we simply turn out backs to the whole green movement? Can Christians today share the world's concern for the earth without compromising their faith?

Yes. But we need to ask God where He wants us. He who created the earth, and wrote the guidelines for its care, longs to show each of us what to do.

He led me to a local group called the Environmental Volunteers—men and women committed to teaching school children to know and care for God's creation. Imagine taking a class of enthusiastic first or second graders on a nature hike along a wooded creek or through a redwood forest. All kinds of hidden mysteries spring to life. Together we explore wonders such as the camouflage colors of lizards, the tiny hooks that "zip up" the slender barbs of a feather, or the biological (not spiritual) interrelationships of various parts of a natural community or ecosystem. In the process, the children learn to respect God's creation, whether they know Him or not.

But before you jump on the environmental bandwagon, and before your children join their school's crusade, you should prepare your family to resist spiritual deception.

W H A T   C A N   F A M I L I E S   D O ?

☐ PRAY!
☐ Know and discuss ...
  1. Key truths about God, the Creator.
  2. Basic facts about the environmental movement.
  3. Blending Christian and pagan beliefs.
  4. Separating helpful information from spiritual deception.

☐ Choose a family project from pages 170–175.

1. KEY TRUTHS ABOUT GOD, THE CREATOR. He is the sovereign Lord of the universe, Fountain of life and Provider for all His creatures. He is the only true source of wisdom and strength. He is our loving Father who embodies all the wise, nurturing characteristics which His opponents link to a mythical spiritual Mother Earth. To those who are willing to follow Him, the earth will reveal not *its own* greatness, but the greatness of its Maker.

☐ Discuss Genesis 1–3; Colossians 1:9-20; Psalms 8, 19, 24.

Since people first gathered together to worship, counterfeit deities have usurped God's place and honor. Consider these names: The Light of the World, Leader of Hosts, Opener of the Womb, Righteous Judge, Lawgiver, Bestower of Strength, Forgiver of Sins.[8] These were attributed not to the sovereign King we know, but to the Goddess Ishtar, the Babylonian "Queen of Heaven" whose beliefs and values are now sweeping across our Western world.

God's adversary, Satan, is a master at switching the message behind familiar words. As usual, he has nothing new to offer—only false images, empty promises, phony solutions, and misleading distortions of God's unfailing, never-changing truth. Therefore, every tempting prize Satan offers us—wisdom, power, a loving Goddess, peace, and a healed earth—are merely costly counterfeits of God's wonderful gifts. Those who reverence creation and "her" occult forces, will find themselves on a downward spiral toward human decadence and earthly decay.

The Bible shows us the consequences of worshiping the earth rather than its Maker:

> Since the creation of the world God's invisible qualities—His eternal power and divine nature—have been clearly seen, being understood from what has been made, so that men are without excuse.
>
> For although they knew God, they neither glorified Him as God nor gave thanks to Him, but their thinking became futile and their foolish hearts were darkened. Although they claimed to be wise, they became fools

... Therefore God gave them over in the sinful desires of their hearts to sexual impurity for the degrading of their bodies with one another. They exchanged the truth of God for a lie, and worshiped and served created things rather than the Creator—who is forever praised *(Romans 1:20-25)*.

God wants His wonder-filled creation to remind us of His majesty, wisdom, and love. *It will, when we want to know Him.* I remember how He showed Himself to me in Norway long ago. With the forest at our doorstep, we children learned early to see God's greatness in a tall tree and a roaring waterfall. Charting our way through the wilderness with a compass, we sensed the marvelous order of His universe. Standing on a barren, windswept mountaintop, we reveled in the splendor of breathtaking scenery. We felt His power in the storms that blew in from the Atlantic. We knew that only a great God could make such a magnificent world. But how did we know?

Years later, after immigrating to America, I found a clue. Wandering through the museum at the Institute of Creation Research in El Cajon, California, I stopped to ponder an exciting poster. Titled simply, "The Principle of Cause and Effect," it explained how creation points to the Creator:

> THE LAW OF CAUSALITY ... states that an effect can never be greater than its cause. A chain of effects and their causes must eventually trace back to an essentially infinite First Cause.
> The First Cause of limitless space must be *infinite*.
> The First Cause of endless time must be *eternal*.
> The First Cause of boundless energy must be *omnipotent*.
> The First Cause of infinite complexity must be *omniscient*.
> The First Cause of infinite love must be *loving*.
> The First Cause of infinite life must be *living*.[9]

It made sense. The First Cause of the universe, the Creator, is our infinite, eternal, all-powerful, all-knowing, personal, holy, loving Father and King!

Around the world, God's people gaze into infinite space on a clear starry night and are amazed by the vastness of His sovereignty. We consider the complexity of a human brain and marvel at the mystery of God's matchless, all-knowing brilliance. We see His ordered and unquenchable life in a world throbbing with tenacious regeneration—even in scorched places like Yellowstone Park after the fiery summer of 1988.

Evidence of His infinite love springs up everywhere: in the fresh waters of a mountain stream, the rich colors of an orchid, the protective hovering of a mother bird. And boundless energy holds everything together. God's creation—His rivers, oceans, winds, and trees—vibrates with the power *He* established in it!

God commissioned His people "to work" His beautiful garden and "take care of it" *(Genesis 2:15)*. He never intended man's authority to become license to greed, gluttony, exploitation, and waste. With the responsibility, He also gave us the capacity to know His heart and be led by His Spirit. He wanted us to view the world through His eyes and care for it with His sensitive wisdom.

But we have hoarded His gifts, wasted many of His resources, and forgotten to thank our Giver. Today we are the losers, just as Israel was millennia ago. Hear the grief in our Father's voice as He ponders man's foolish ways: "I brought you into a fertile land to eat its fruit and rich produce. But you came and defiled My land and made My inheritance detestable" *(Jeremiah 2:7)*.

2. BASIC FACTS ABOUT THE ENVIRONMENTAL MOVEMENT. The Green Movement is man's effort to turn the tide of waste and degradation. It is also a complex and changing network of groups loosely joined through a common vision: to restore social, political, and ecological justice to the world. No small order! It calls its members Greens in appreciation for a thriving, green outdoors. Spreading around the world, it includes radical left Greens, antinuclear Greens, visionary/holistic Greens, Social Greens, single issue Greens, ecofeminist Greens, Native American Greens. Some

lists even include red Greens, supposedly marxist Greens or lukewarm politicians who merely claim to be Green. More militant Greens compare them to watermelons: green on the outside, red on the inside. Most groups fit loosely into three categories:

☐ Conservation. This includes long-standing organizations like The Audubon Society, The Nature Conservancy, and the National Wildlife Federation, which traditionally have emphasized land preservation rather than political action.

☐ Social Greens are politically active organizations such as Greenpeace and Earth First! Rooted in the counterculture movement of the 1960s, they lean toward the political left. Their agenda usually reaches far beyond ecology to rights for women and gays, nuclear disarmament, and economic redistribution based on socialist philosophies.

☐ Deep Ecology views Gaia as the divine center and source of all life. It has added a spiritual dimension to the *Gaia* hypothesis developed by British scientist Dr. James Lovelock, who views the earth as a wise, self-guiding, self-sustaining organism. The Deeps or Spiritual Greens tell us that Earth can save herself—she has the wisdom and power; humans don't. But we can help her by becoming conscious of the oneness and sacredness of all her parts. Deeps criticize Social Greens for their "shallow" motive: saving the earth for humanity's sake rather than for Mother Earth herself. Key spokespeople are Thomas Berry, controversial Dominican priest Matthew Fox, and physicist Fritjof Capra, author of *The Tao of Physics*, who makes even Eastern mysticism sound scientific.

The distinctions between the above categories are fading. Many Conservationists and Social Greens have recognized the motivating force of religious convictions and are embracing Deep Ecology. Deep Ecologists and Conservationists see the need for political power to enforce their objectives. It is no surprise that the National Wildlife Federation has formed a partnership with John Denver's Windstar—a

Colorado based educational center that trains teachers in mystical, evolutionary New Age globalism as well as practical ecology.

Greens in all three categories generally agree on one point: Today's ecological crisis is rooted in Christian traditions.[10] They tell us:

☐ The Judeo/Christian belief that God assigned man to "rule over" the earth has caused us to exploit and abuse it.
☐ Monotheism (one God) separated humans from their ancient connection to the earth. To reverse the trend, storytellers and artists must revive earth-centered myth and reconnect us to Earth's spirit.
☐ The diversity of species enriches the earth. Healthy, flourishing diversity requires a substantial decrease in the human population and its interference with nature's processes.
☐ Heavenly minded Christians care little for a temporary earth.
☐ By resisting the return of earth-centered religions, Christians block the global movement toward the one-world religion needed to unify people and save the earth.

As Christians, we need to prayerfully consider *God's* guidelines and let Him show us where we have misused His resources. But we do not need to accept the role of a scapegoat or apologize for our beliefs. Later chapters will show that the solution proposed by Deep Ecology—a speedy return to paganism—will only multiply the earth's distress.

Elliot Miller, in *A Crash Course on the New Age Movement*, defines our challenge:

> Undeniably, the earth has suffered much abuse under the pretext of biblical sanction. Human greed often twists Scripture to suit its own ends. The answer to this regrettable situation is not to abandon biblical truth for pagan mythology. We must recover a biblical appreciation for creation and man's role in it, without falling into the opposite and more damning error of worshiping the creature rather than the Creator.[11]

3. BLENDING CHRISTIAN AND PAGAN BELIEFS. In the spring of 1990, a conference brochure that came in the mail looked promising at first glance; yet, the discordant blend of workshop titles disturbed me: "Healing Mother Earth," "The Sacredness of Nature," "Christian Environmental Ethics," "Cosmic Creativity." Was this North American Conference on Christianity and Ecology (NACCE) really Christian?

To find out, I joined a crowd of enthusiastic Greens in San Francisco. Prepared to resist the pantheistic spiritism so prevalent in the Green movement, I prayed for encounters with those whose attitudes toward nature echoed the heart of the Creator.

God answered quickly. Warmly welcomed by coordinator Frederick Krueger, I showed him another mailing I recently received from the North American Conference on *Religion* and Ecology. I had noticed that the names of two organizations differ by one word: one emphasizes Christianity, the other, religion.

"Is there a connection between the NACCE and the NACRE?" I asked, pointing to the announcement of a Washington, D.C. conference. Featuring England's Prince Philip, it promised that "environmental theology will be in the '90s ... what liberation theology has been to Third World countries in the '80s."

"We split," explained Krueger. "They wanted to replace the word *Christianity* with *Religion* in order to include Buddhism and Hinduism. We wanted to remain Christian."

"Thank you for taking that stand," I said, feeling a growing appreciation for this dedicated defender of God's handiwork, but wondering what he meant by *Christian*.

Passing a row of display tables on my way to the auditorium, I gathered an armload of literature ranging from lists of practical conservation measures to a puzzling vow: "I pledge allegiance to the heart of Our Mother Earth ... " I also bought the April issue of Matthew Fox's *Creation* magazine, wondering how his mystical view of God's creation could fit into a supposedly Christian setting.

I sat down, opened *Creation,* and read Fox's introductory statement: "Our goal is to bring out the wisdom and mystery of the cosmos itself as celebrated by today's sciences and the wisdom of Western mystics, primal people and artists."[12] An excerpt from *The Language of the Goddess* by Dr. Marija Gimbutas praised the cultural richness and sacred rituals of the Goddess ("*I am* she that is the natural mother of all things . . . chief of the powers divine")[13] who, centuries ago, hid underground to escape "oppression from male-dominated societies." Did she mean Christian ones?

I tried another publication, NACCE's own quarterly, *Firmament*. What a contrast! A delightful quote caught my eye: "Love of the Earth should be the natural overflow of a Christ-centered life."[14]

The conference opened with an ecumenical bouquet of prayers and a prerecorded video message from David Brower, founder of Earth Island Institute. He urged us to work "shoulder to shoulder" even with people we disagree with, to put "back together the life-support system that the Creator gave us."

For the rest of the day, the spiritual focus swung like a pendulum in and out of biblical truth. One session taught the divinity of all things. (In Genesis 3:17 and Romans 8:20-21, God declares the opposite.) Another session acknowledged the transcendence of our Creator. A workshop called "Universal Kinship: Brother Sun and Sister Moon" affirmed monism (all is one) while "Scripture and Environmental Principles" offered helpful biblical guidelines.

The conference ended with biblical truth. William Dyrness, then Dean at New College, Berkeley, taught "Stewardship of the Land in the Biblical Tradition" to enthusiastic listeners, while Fred Krueger led a workshop encouraging us to practice the disciplines of a God-centered life.

Driving home I reviewed the day. I had heard some strange teaching, but unlike other Green groups I had encountered, the NACCE welcomed Christians. Yes, many seemed to confuse biblical truth with pagan religions. Yet, most participants hungered for God's guidelines, and *everyone* longed to pitch in and clean up God's creation. No apathy here!

One thing was clear: To join any environmental group today requires spiritual discernment. But so does simply living in our fast-changing culture. Schools, the media, movies, and peers bring us (especially our children) face to face with a tempting array of spiritual counterfeits. Some sound *almost* like truth. But isn't that the nature of a counterfeit? It always tries to hide its deception behind an enticing imitation of truth.

Does your family know the genuine well enough to discern the counterfeit?

4. SEPARATING HELPFUL INFORMATION FROM SPIRITUAL DECEPTION. Sometimes it seems that nature worshipers—Buddhist monks, Native American shamans, witchdoctors—put Christians to shame by their devotion. Practicing the discipline of stillness and the art of listening, they model a commitment God longs to see in His own people. Yet, by rejecting their Maker, they oppose the very purpose for which He created the earth they love—to manifest *His* glory.

God's path to healing of the earth is written in the Bible, not in the well-meaning but distorted philosophies of earth-centered reformers. To test an environmental philosophy, ask yourself these questions: Does it agree with Scripture and honor God? Or does it focus on the creation and deny its Maker? Or does it blend truth and error?

If we keep thanking God for the wonders of His creation, we will also share His concern for the land and its life—and He cares about the smallest detail. Remember, even the death of a sparrow touches His gentle heart, and the wasteful destruction of a single fruit tree belittles His wonderful gift and hinders His plan *(Deuteronomy 20:19-20)*. This kind of stewardship demands a wisdom and love that far exceeds our meager supply. But God wants our inadequacy to drive us to Him, so that He can demonstrate His sufficiency in and through us. "My grace is sufficient for you," He says, "for My power is made perfect in weakness" *(2 Corinthians 12:9)*.

God can use the environmental movement to teach us to respect and enjoy nature. But since most environmentalists reject the biblical Creator, *we need to filter everything they tell us through biblical truth.* This practice, fed by daily reading of

Chart 1: THREE VIEWS OF THE EARTH © 1992 Berit Kjos		
DEEP ECOLOGY (Biocentric)	HUMANIST GREEN ACTIVISM (Anthropocentric)	CHRISTIAN STEWARDSHIP (Theocentric)
Earth-centered	Human-centered	God-centered
Mother Earth evolved, and nurtures and organizes her parts	Earth and man evolved by chance	God created the earth and its inhabitants
Human animals are conscious expressions of Mother Earth	Human animals are responsible for Earth	God told His people to use and care for Earth
Wisdom from Nature	Wisdom for self	Wisdom from God (Bible)
Connect with Gaia through ritual, celebration, drugs, meditation, sex	Connect with nature through human mind, emotions, experience	Commune with God through prayer, praise, biblical meditation
Help Earth save herself by hearing her spirit and heeding her wisdom (spiritism)	Save Earth by trusting human nature	Care for Earth by trusting God's Word, receiving His strength and guidance

God's Word, gives us freedom to go wherever God leads us and to enjoy all that He shows us.

This kind of freedom may bring us in contact with all sorts of beliefs. One morning I hiked through a redwood forest near San Francisco with a leader in the Green movement who was also an elementary school teacher. Love for nature and a desire for simplicity had brought us together for this moment, though we were poles apart spiritually. She told me that she was a lesbian and a witch.

Her spiritual connection with the ancient Goddess came as no surprise. In my studies, I had already noticed the amazing correlation between Deep Ecology, ecofeminism (a blend of ecology, emphasis on sensuality, and feminine spirituality) and witchcraft. Silently I reaffirmed the Armor of God which I had put on that morning (see chapter 2). Then I continued to hear—and appreciate—this woman's deep concern for the well-being of the earth, its animals, the homeless, and the poverty stricken children in her class-room. Was I as willing to serve His hurting ones?

"Since you love nature, wouldn't Matthew Fox's Chris-tianity be more relevant for you?" asked the witch, referring to my biblical beliefs.

"I looked through his book, *The Coming of the Cosmic Christ,*" I answered. "Fox describes a different Jesus—not the personal Jesus I know and love."

We listened to the whispers of the wind in the treetops and they reminded me of Psalm 96:12, "All the trees of the forest will sing for joy." Perhaps they reminded her of what she believed—the spiritual connectedness of all things.

"I pray when I sense God's presence," I said. "Do you pray to the Goddess?"

"No," she answered. "We don't pray. We call it 'doing magic.' "

I shivered as I thought about her words. *Self-will, mind control, earthy spirits.* The occult formula for magic seemed puny compared to the infinite might of the God who creat-ed these towering redwoods. The King who reigns over His creation, yet lives in His people, is immeasurably "greater than the one who is in the world" *(1 John 4:4).* In the pres-ence of His majesty, man's arrogant dreams and grandiose plans seem absurd. Only our sovereign Maker can heal the earth. He determines its destiny. As He shows us the ways to responsible stewardship, we should follow Him, and remember the true song of the earth; "Let everything that has breath praise the LORD!" *(Psalm 150:6)*

Calling the
Spirit of Gaia

The call is to serve the well-being of the living planet,
Gaia . . . to enter into a holistic consciousness.
—Barry McWaters, psychologist[1]

The more you contact the voice of the living Earth and
evaluate what it says, the easier it will become for you to
contact it and trust what it provides.
—The Sierra Club's sourcebook,
Well Body, Well Earth[2]

*Turn . . . to the living God who made heaven and earth. (Acts
14:15)*

SOFT, HYPNOTIC MUSIC greeted the parents streaming into the
kindergarten classroom for a back-to-school orientation. The
teacher was preparing a special journey—via guided imagery. She focused everyone's attention on a poster which
showed doors of every size, shape, and color. As she began
the visualization, her voice turned meditative and
mysterious.

> Imagine that you are standing at one of the doors. In
> just a moment the door will open and you will walk
> in. (Pause)
> The door has opened and you are standing at the
> top of a stairway. Now, as I count, picture yourself
> walking down the stairs—ten, nine, eight, seven. . . .
> You are at the bottom of the stairs, standing in a

beautiful valley. It is green, lush, and you are walking along a path. Along the side of the path you notice a milkweed plant, and as you look closer you see a cater-pillar.... Now *you become the caterpillar. You* keep eating and eating.... *You* get very tired. *You* spin a co-coon around yourself and rest....

Now *you* have become a wonderful monarch butter-fly. *You* are flying around . . . through a rainbow. . . .[3]

That seemed innocent enough. But was it? After the exercise, only one couple expressed concern. This relatively mild hypnotic exercise encouraged the rest of the parents to re-lax, *feel* their supposed connectedness with related animal species—and build resistance against future concern over similar or more occult visualizations.

I am not suggesting we starve our imaginations or quench our tendencies to visualize. We couldn't if we tried. The imagination forms mental images all day long—when-ever we hear a story, remember an event, or read a book. God uses it to reveal Himself to us when we study His Word.

But who or what guides our imagination? There are four possibilities: God, self, another person, or demonic spirit guides. Few realize that human guides, manipulating the imagination through hypnotic visualizations, can produce an altered state of consciousness that opens the mind to occult suggestions. Satan never tires of twisting God's good gifts to fit his schemes.

> The practice of visualization, or "directed imagination," is part of all forms of occultism, ancient as well as modern. . . . The ability to form clear, detailed, mental images is the key to unlocking occult powers, and visualization is the basis for in-voking any deity or spiritual being.[4]

Seeking the Spirit of Gaia.

Oneness, harmony, contact with earth's wisdom . . . the promised fruit of earth-centered spirituality—these sound refreshing to our self-focused, power-hungry generation.

Unaware of the dangers, the educational establishment and a growing number of parents are encouraging this "new" spiritual awareness and applauding classroom exercises that "empower" children to sense their oneness with the earth and her other species.

Today's visionaries tell us that such spiritual connectedness is the earth's only hope. In *The Dream of the Earth,* Thomas Berry summarized the world's dilemma—and his answer:

> Human administration of the universe in any comprehensive manner is far too great a task.... What we need ... is the sensitivity to understand and respond to the psychic energies deep in the very structure of reality itself.... This is the ultimate wisdom of tribal peoples.[5]

The Sierra Club Environmental Health Sourcebook, *Well Body, Well Earth* by Mike Samuels and Hal Zina Bennett, shows us how. It tells us to "turn to the traditions of ancient cultures" such as Buddhist meditations and Native American Hopi rituals in order to "reaffirm our bond with the spirit of the living earth":

> The practice of visualization, that is, deliberately using your imagination to focus your attention on a particular goal, is an important mental tool for change ... [and] probably dates back to human beginnings.... In Greece, for example, when people wanted help in solving difficult problems, they consulted the Oracle at Delphi. [There] the priests acknowledged a spirit of the living Earth for which the Greek name was Gaea. Priestesses of Gaea were trained in the art of visualization and had dedicated their lives to a study of the spirit of the living Earth. When asked to help a person solve a problem—such as when to plant their fields or how to influence the conception of children—the priestess ... imagined herself consulting with Gaea. The answer coming from the visualization of Gaea was the answer the priestess gave....

The visualization exercises we describe here are intended to help people focus on the concept of the living Earth. Because most people who live in an urban or suburban setting have little or no daily contact with the Earth, we require something like visualization to help us get in touch with our planet....[6]

Well Body, Well Earth details the steps (deep breathing, relaxation and autosuggestions) to "the level of consciousness" where "you can be in touch with those forces in the universe that... encourage health and well-being."[7] Here in a trance state, you are ready to visualize the creation of the universe—even to have a dialogue with Mother Earth herself.

"The more you contact the voice of the living Earth," promise the authors, "the easier it will become for you to contact it and trust what it provides."[8]

There is no doubt that the last statement is true. The more a person deals with earthy spirits, the more tenaciously they cling. While God speaks through one Holy Spirit, "the voice" of Earth comes from armies of demons. The seeker who follows the above advice may become deaf to God and host to an oppressive parasitic demon that some versions of the Bible call *a familiar spirit*. Only God's authority and power can bring freedom.[9]

Psychics, channelers, witches and shamans (tribal medicine men) know that occult forces may loose hidden terrors. Some have issued strong warnings against naive experimentation which may invoke mischievous, even murderous, spirits. But their warnings have failed to stop environmental pied pipers; speaking from some of the most influential platforms in our nations, they promote earthy spirituality and occult connections with evangelistic zeal.

Eco-Education.

One such enthusiast, Andy LePage, wrote a book that seems to be doing what its title promises: *Transforming Education* (1987). Its long list of endorsers includes notables like Matthew Fox and Dr. Robert Muller, former under secretary of the United Nation's Economic and Social Council.

"Andy LePage's book," says Muller, "opens the curtain on one of the most exciting and promising philosophical educational debates there ever was on this planet."[10]

What planetary philosophy does LePage teach? Like others who promote a speedy return to nature worship, he emphasizes the need to discard the "disease of *dualism*"[11] (dividing reality into two opposing forces—the physical versus the spiritual). He challenges educators to awaken students to their oneness with the entire creation (monism) through models such as Hatha Yoga, witchcraft, and Native American spiritism.[12]

But do educators really buy this religious dogma? Indeed, many do, with all their heart.

"Andy LePage has written what may well become one of the most important books in education," says Professor Sidney B. Simon, father of values clarification, "which should be given to every new teacher, every new principal, and certainly, to every new school board member. Should that happen, the education of our children would take a turn for the better that might be enough to save us all."[13]

Since LePage wrote his book, a growing assortment of environmental curricula has flooded classrooms. I *hope* much of it presents practical information untouched by the persuasions of Deep Ecology. Children need to know ecological *facts* and be encouraged toward environmental wisdom—but not its spirituality. A 1990 *Wall Street Journal* article shared nationwide expressions of enthusiasm for earth stewardship.

> No figures are available, but thousands of schools across the country have worked environmentalism into the classroom, usually in science courses but also in social studies, English and other subjects. Florida, Maryland and Iowa are among states interested in a five-year-old law in Wisconsin that required public schools from kindergarten to twelfth grade, to integrate ecology into the curriculum. . . . Congress is considering a bill that would fashion and make available an environmental-studies program for schools around the country.[14]

It sounds good. Yet, teaching on environmental awareness often includes political, economic, cultural and spiritual persuasions that neither children nor parents are prepared to evaluate. For example, how should students (and parents) respond when a classroom cassette tape intones the rhythmic sounds of Native American prayers to Mother Earth? Or when a schoolwide Earth Fest engages the students in "water cycle dances" — something that happened in a Pennsylvania school?[15]

Once we know the sources of much of our environmental curricula, we can help our children to discern spiritual counterfeits. Much of this curriculum flows from the New Age/Deep Ecology philosophies of John Denver's Colorado-based Windstar and Steve Van Matre's Institute for Earth Education in Illinois. The demand for their curriculum is soaring. According to the article, "Education That Cannot Wait" by Mike Weilbacher, Van Matre may be "the most creative force" in environmental education:

> Van Matre's work has been replicated planet wide; his activities form the backbone of many nature center programs.
>
> Once, environmental educators begged to be let inside the schools. Today teachers are banging on the front doors of nature centers.[16]

What does Van Matre believe? "This," he says, referring to a portion of his book *The Earth Speaks*, "is about giving up old ways of seeing, about loving the earth as a whole, about tapping into the universal flow of life . . . "[17]

Let's cage ourselves and let the animals run free.
Let's tear down our egocentric structures . . . and build anew.
Let's find new stars and new songs to follow.
Let's build some foundations under our dreams. (Steve Van Matre)[18]

Curriculum that takes students beyond objective reality

and opens the door to earth-centered spirituality can be divided into three categories:

☐ Training students to connect with earth's life force.
☐ Reinstating earth-centered myth as a guiding force.
☐ Teaching practical witchcraft and mind control.

While some of the illustrations in this and the next two chapters may not sound like environmental teaching, they encourage students to discard traditional views of reality and to accept the pagan perspective (paradigm) essential to Deep Ecology. Notice that the beliefs and practices of spiritism (communicating with demonic spirits), witchcraft, and shamanism (using magic to contact various spirits) fit right into ancient nature worship. According to their promoters, these steps will help our children connect with the earth, with their supposedly divine inner selves, and with each other. They will empower them to rebuild their sick, polluted world.

Training in Spiritism.
Like every earth-based culture before us, America is tapping into occult forces that blind people to God's truth. It doesn't matter whether we call the force Mother Earth, Gaia, psychic power, or cosmic energy; all point to the same unholy source. Satan's power may be puny compared to the might of our sovereign King, but it is far greater than mere human strength. And the most vulnerable among us, our children, face the greatest onslaught.

Schools have adopted age-old pagan formulas to teach self-esteem and personal empowerment. For example, "Pumsy in Pursuit of Excellence," a controversial self-esteem program used in "more than 12,000 elementary schools nationwide"[19] uses a cute dragon puppet to train students in self-hypnosis. Presented as a "cognitive, mental health curriculum,"[20] it trains children to use relaxation exercises, visualizations, and chants to create their own meadow, float through the air on Pumsy's back, meet and speak with Pumsy's friend, feel strength coming into their bodies...

That occult indoctrination can happen on a grand scale

was proven during 1989–1990, when teachers in seventy Los Angeles schools introduced children to their personal spirit guides. Two thousand children, third grade and up, participated in the pilot program, Mission SOAR—"Set Objectives, Achieve Results." Bob Simonds, President of *Citizens for Excellence in Education* (CEE), alerted parents through a newsletter with the following information:

> The lessons in Mission SOAR parallel closely . . . the exercises outlined in the New Age book, *Beyond Hypnosis: A Program For Developing Your Psychic and Healing Power*, by leading New Age psychic William H. Hewitt. Children . . . are hypnotized, introduced to demonic spirits, and told to seek "their counsel" when making decisions. Hard to believe?[21]

This outline of the exercises taught in the program shows the most familiar steps to occult connectedness and oppression:

☐ Prehypnotic preparation through relaxation
☐ Hypnotic control through colors (visualizing a rainbow)
☐ Breaking the hypnotic spell
☐ Conjuring up the dead, summoning spirit guides
☐ Creating an inner psychic room to meet spirits
☐ Learning that psychic medicine will cure all illnesses
☐ Accepting the spirit beings into your life
☐ Receiving psychic power from a white light, a common element in contemporary psychic communication (2 *Corinthians 11:14*)
☐ Planning one's life with the help of spirit guides. "Your helpers are both experts and can help you, teach you, guide you, listen to you, and counsel you at anytime . . . Know that [he and she] will always be there at your side whenever you need [them]."[22]

A Girl Scout camporee director led about forty junior scouts (ages 10–12) on a similar journey. According to a concerned California scout leader who observed the campfire ceremony, the director, dressed as a Native American, invoked the Great Spirit and the spirits of the woods, the North, South, East, and West. After explaining their entrance into womanhood and marking their foreheads with ashes, she led the girls on a meditational journey to contact the earth and a personal spirit guide. "Imagine a meadow ..." intoned her mysterious voice. "See a young woman sitting under a tree. Talk to her." This wise person would be their life companion and helper.

With such constant and faithful spirit helpers, who would want to follow advice from Mom, Dad, or God? Why invite a contrary opinion when the guide speaks what one wants to hear—at least in the beginning?

The Apostle Paul warned us that "in later times some will abandon the faith and follow deceiving spirits and things taught by demons" (1 Timothy 4:1). Spiritual experimentation, whether in the name of ecology, globalism or self-realization, yields confusion instead of wisdom, fear instead of self-confidence, and bondage instead of freedom. Each such program results in wasted teaching time, erosion of biblical beliefs and values, and the possibility of devastating mental and spiritual oppression.

Contrary to Satan's glowing promises, spiritism hinders rather than helps us live peaceably with the earth. God told us so! His warning to Israel rings true for us today:

> Let no one be found among you who ... practices divination or sorcery, interprets omens, engages in witchcraft, or casts spells, or who is a medium or spiritist or who consults the dead. ... Because of these detestable practices the Lord your God will drive out those nations (Deuteronomy 18:10-12).

WHAT CAN FAMILIES DO?

☐ PRAY for wisdom from the *Holy* Spirit.
☐ Prepare your family to resist counterfeit spirits.
  1. Know the role of the Holy Spirit in your life.
  2. Join together with other families.
  3. Put on the Armor of God (Ephesians 6:10-18).
  4. Enjoy your Father's world.
☐ Choose a family project from the list on pages 170–175.

1. KNOW THE ROLE OF THE HOLY SPIRIT IN YOUR LIFE. Discuss the following verses: John 3:5-6, 34-35; John 14:16-17, 26; John 16:7-14; Acts 1:8 (power to accomplish God's will, not our demands); 1 John 4:2, 13.

2. JOIN TOGETHER WITH OTHER FAMILIES. Today's battle for children's minds and biblical values is primarily spiritual. We cannot fight the rising tide of counterfeit spirituality alone. In *Your Child and the New Age,* I have described a course of action that begins with prayer, is sustained by ongoing communication with God and confidence in His Word, and is accomplished as Christian families seek God's direction and victory together. I encourage you to read it.

If the Holy Spirit prompts you to speak to local educators, consider the following steps:

☐ Ask God to help you build a Christian support group that prays and works together. Many occult exercises throughout the country (including the meditations in Michigan and Los Angeles) were discontinued after parents prayed, joined together, and explained to schools that such activities are illegal.

☐ When approaching a teacher or school officials, trust God to speak the truth *in love (Ephesians 4:15)* through you. Begin by expressing understanding for the school's goals and appreciation for genuine efforts. As an ambassador for His kingdom, reflect His love, wisdom, and patience—not fear, hostility, and a self-righteous attitude. Many teachers have been won to Christ by the loving concern of a Christian parent.

☐ *Citizens for Excellence in Education* can provide helpful information about the problem you face, the best way to confront school officials and your legal alternatives. While countless wonderful teachers still hold back the rising tide of counterfeit spirituality in their schools, the educational establishment now trains others to resist "fundamentalist" Christians who oppose *their* agenda. We need to stand together. Contact the CEE/NACE at P.O. Box 3200, Costa Mesa, California 92628.

3. PUT ON THE ARMOR OF GOD. Young and old members of God's family need to embrace wise environmentalism but to reject pagan spirituality. I know no better way to nurture discernment between these than by putting on our spiritual armor as outlined in Ephesians 6:10-18.

God showed our family that to resist deception, each of us needed to know truth and to be alert to the enemy's tricks. The essential first step involved family Bible study— filling, renewing, and protecting our minds with truth. We began to read and discuss a psalm and a chapter a day. Then, using truth as our filter and guide, we could take a closer look at the counterfeit.

In *Screwtape Letters,* C.S. Lewis tells about two "equal and opposite errors" that undermine our defense against deception and therefore delight Satan and his invisible armies: "One is to disbelieve in their existence. The other is to believe, and to feel an excessive and unhealthy interest in them."[23]

Demonstrating a healthy balance, Paul's letter to the Ephesians gives us five chapters of information about God, His grace, and His ways before it exposes our adversary. Finally, in chapter 6, verse 12, Paul tells us that "Our struggle is not against flesh and blood, but against the *rulers,* against the *authorities,* against the *powers* of this dark world and against the *spiritual forces of evil* in the heavenly realms."

The commander of this spiritual army is Satan. Masquerading as an angel of light, he began to work on Eve soon after Creation, by causing her to *doubt* God's word: "Did God really say...?" And by promising a *tempting alternative:* "When you eat of it your eyes will be opened, and you will be like God, knowing good and evil" *(Genesis 3:1-5).* Today he still lures people with enticing offers of higher knowledge and oneness with God.

Our family made a striking discovery. The *full armor* worn and wielded provides an outline of essential truths that enable us to discern all kinds of deception. These truths parallel all the popular lies of Deep Ecology, neopaganism and the New Age movement. In other words, when we know, trust, and speak the truths of the armor, they will expose and counter every deception.

To put on the armor, we review and we affirm each of the essential truths, starting with the truth about God Himself. Trusting the Holy Spirit to make these truths living and active in us *(Hebrews 4:12)*, we pray something like this:

☐ TRUTH. Thank You, God, for showing me the truth about Yourself and Your ways.

☐ RIGHTEOUSNESS. Thank You, Jesus, for giving me Your righteousness. I can't please You on my own, but You live in me, and Your life is perfect. (We also confess our sins, remembering God's promise in *1 John 1:9*.)

☐ PEACE. Thank You for Your peace in me. Filled with Your righteous life, I have peace to share with others—no matter what.

☐ FAITH. Lord, I choose to count on Your promises and follow Your Word today.

☐ SALVATION. I trust You to lead me safely today and forever.

☐ SWORD, GOD'S WORD. Show me which Scriptures I need to know and affirm in order to triumph in every battle I face today. (Our favorite: *Galatians 2:20*.)

Does the armor *really* keep us safe? Yes, as long as we keep wearing *every* part. But keep in mind, putting on the armor is not simply a formula to follow. It is a daily commitment to seek, study, and follow Truth—Jesus Christ Himself. When you know and acknowledge Him, and follow the path He has shown you to Himself (through confession, repentance, and the work of the cross), He protects you. For Christ, who is Himself the armor and all its parts, is the One who covers you even as He fills you with His own life *(John 14:20; Romans 13:14; Psalm 32:7)*.

We can count on Him! Many years ago, as a new Christian, I went to a holistic therapist for help with my back. "Polarity balances the positive and negative energies of your body," she had told me. But I felt uneasy—especially when I noticed a mystical picture on the wall.

"Who is he?" I asked cautiously.

"That's my priest. He's like a spirit guide."

"I'm a Christian," I said. "I get my strength from God.

Chart 2: THE ARMOR OF GOD		
© 1992 Berit Kjos		
	CHRISTIANITY	*EARTH-BASED SPIRITUALITY*
Belt of TRUTH	*God is . . .* our loving Father (John 3:16) all-powerful King (1 Tim. 1:17) the only God (Deut. 4:39) far greater than His creation	*Earth* (Gaia, goddess) *is . . .* a living, feminine force divine source of power & wisdom in all *(Pantheism)* one with all *(Monism)*
Breastplate of RIGHTEOUS-NESS	*We are . . .* God's creation (Psalm 100:3), children, ambassadors, friends naturally selfish (Rom. 3:23) righteous when we receive life of Jesus by faith (Gal. 2:20) led by God	*We are . . .* part of Gaia, connected to all her other parts naturally good, sacred perfect when in harmony with nature in control of ourselves
Walking in PEACE	*Therefore we have peace . . .* with God (Rom. 5:1) through Jesus, "our peace" (Eph. 2:14) to share (John 20:21)	*We have harmony . . .* with earth, her rhythms through TM, visualization, guided imagery . . . to teach others
Shield of FAITH	*Faith means choosing to . . .* trust God (Mark 11:22) count on truth, facts, what we already have *in Christ* follow His Word (Rom. 4:18-21)	*Faith means choosing to . . .* grow in consciousness trust natural thoughts, spirits, dreams, images . . . follow dreams and desires
Helmet of SALVATION	*We triumph* (are saved) by Christ's life in us counting on His promises for today (Rom. 8:28, 37) for eternity (1 Thes. 4:17)	*We triumph by . . .* connecting with the Earth empowering ourselves for today rebirth and reincarnation (rebut with Heb. 9:27)
Sword of the Spirit, GOD'S WORD	*We speak God's Word* (Heb. 4:12)	*We speak* and project mental images, do magic

Where do you get your power?"

"From my spirit guide." A coolness had crept into her

voice. "It's the energy of the universe, but it comes through my guide into my hands and then into you."

Into me? Though I had put on the armor that morning, I quickly affirmed each part again. I continued to pray that God Himself would shield me from any occult power operating through the Vita's hands.

He did! As soon as she touched my back, she began to cough. Her body shook until she moved away from me.

"What are you doing?" I asked.

"Realigning my energies," she explained.

But the moment she tried to start the massage, another attack of coughing stopped her. Frustrated and angry, she announced what I already knew. "I can't work on you. My power won't enter your field of energy."

I tried to explain that God had protected me, but she didn't want to hear. Thankful that my Lord had demonstrated His power to both of us, I drove home. Once again He had proven that He who lives in me, "is greater than he who is in the world" *(1 John 4:4).*

4. ENJOY YOUR FATHER'S WORLD. We don't need a mystical host of guides and spirits to show us God's creation. If we ask, the Holy Spirit will open our eyes to enjoy God's wonders. He wants to use those wonders to show us the Creator Himself.

When the crowds pressed and the demands seemed unending, Jesus often sought solitude and strength on a quiet mountainside or by the shore of Galilee. There He would talk with His Father and receive wisdom and strength for the day. "Come with Me by yourselves," He invites each of us, "to a quiet place and get some rest" *(Mark 6:31).*

It's not easy to find time or solitude in our hectic, high-pressured lifestyles. If I had to catch up on all obligations first, it would never happen. Yet, when I make time to meet my Lord in one of the special places He has shown me, His quieting strength more than compensates.

When my sons were younger, we often explored the nearby park. We would ask God to show us something special—small or large, ordinary as a trail of laboring ants or extraordinary as a bird feeding her babies—that would demonstrate His love, order, and creativity.

Sometimes we would simply lie on our backs and gaze up into the leafy crowns of surrounding trees. We would close our eyes, listen to nature's sounds, and thank our Shepherd for His wonderful presence. Unlike Eastern meditation (where one empties the mind, then welcomes any spiritual voice willing to fill it), this time of stillness sharpened our minds—and filled our thoughts with God's *words, works, and wonders.*

Author and nature guide Joseph Cornell has helped thousands of people—young and old—to know and enjoy nature. He also demonstrates the two-sided thrust of the environmental movement: practical help and occult spirituality. In *Sharing Nature with Children,* he suggests several ways you can build respect and love for nature in yourself and others. His five points on "How To Be an Effective Nature Guide" remind *us* as adults to slow down and tune our hearts to the Creator's own art.

    ☐ Teach less, and share more.
    ☐ Be receptive. Receptivity means listening. Be alert. Something exciting or interesting is almost always happening.
    ☐ Focus the child's attention without delay. Involve everyone as much as you can, by asking questions and pointing out interesting sights and sounds...
    ☐ Look and experience first; talk later. Observe the tree from unusual perspectives. Feel and smell its bark and leaves. Quietly sit on or under its branches, and be aware of all the forms of life that live in and around the tree and depend on it.
    ☐ A sense of joy should permeate the experience. Remember that your own enthusiasm is contagious.[24]

Sharing Nature with Children has been endorsed by the National Audubon Society as "a powerful tool in educating children," the National Science Teachers Association, and the Boy Scouts and Girl Scouts of America. The foreword by Paul E. Knoop, Jr., Program Director at the National Audubon Society's Aullwood Center, tells about Joseph Cornell's participation in their Naturalist Training Program:

> The Aullwood staff were taken by Joseph's naturalness and love for the earth. When he was in the outdoors, it was obvious that Joseph was in his element: he spoke to the trees, touched them with love—and, yes, even embraced them. He had a childlike quality, and it always seemed to him the earth was a place of beauty and mystery.[25]

Sound good? But wait a moment! Before you run out and buy one of his best-sellers, let me share something else about Joseph Cornell. This inspiring nature lover belongs to the Ananda World Brotherhood Village, a cozy community nestled in the foothills of California's Sierra mountains. Sri Kriyananda, founder and spiritual director of Ananda, was discipled by Indian yoga master, Paramhansa Yogananda, who came to America to "awaken" Hindu spirituality.

Ananda satellite groups adorn suburban centers and university campuses with posters inviting the public to a delicious assortment of spiritual treats: Self-Realization, Attunement, Meditation.

In *Listening to Nature,* Cornell paints a panorama with quotes from various pagan teachers. Black Elk's Native American spirituality exposes the heart of Deep Ecology: "Peace... comes within the souls of people when they realize... their oneness with the universe and all its powers, and when they realize that at the center of the universe dwells the Great Spirit, and that this center is really everywhere."[26]

Unfortunately, Cornell's enticing blend of delightful insights, heartfelt devotion, and spiritual deception characterizes much of the environmental movement. Please don't misunderstand—I'm not suggesting we therefore dismiss all of the movement's literature or avoid Green groups. For example, the Audubon Society continues to deepen my appreciation and concern for God's wonderful creatures—and may be oblivious of Cornell's spiritual persuasions. *Ask God* to show you to His choice of books—then read with discernment, wear the armor, and trust your Shepherd to guide your family as you follow Him.

THREE

Myths, Magic, Mysticism, and Make-Believe

We ... need to reawaken something very old ... our understanding of Earth wisdom. We need to accept the invitation to the dance—the dance of unity of humans, plants, animals, the Earth.
>   —Bill Devall and George Sessions, *Deep Ecology*[1]

The images of myth are reflections of the spiritual potentialities of every one of us. Through contemplating these, we evoke their powers in our own lives.
>   —Joseph Campbell, *The Power of Myth*[2]

The time will come when men will not put up with sound doctrine. Instead, to suit their own desires, they will gather around them a great number of teachers to say what their itching ears want to hear. They will turn their ears away from the truth and turn aside to myths. (2 Timothy 4:3-4)

"MOM, LOOK IN THIS WINDOW." Our son David pointed to a strange figure of a woman in the store next to our family's favorite Chinese restaurant. "It's called the Deer Maiden."

Forgetting food for a moment, we stopped to gaze at the fascinating display in the *Earth Visions* window. The four-foot figure of the Deer Maiden looked like a contemporary blend of goddess and shaman. Clothed in layers of fur, feathers, velvet, and lace, she smiled seductively at us. Sprigs of dried flowers and herbs adorned her hair, filled her hands, and flowed down on a little sign by her bare, bejeweled feet. The sign said,

Deep in the ancient woods hidden by the ferns, the Deer Maiden pauses. She blends the best of us—animal and man—and speaks of promises and of tomorrows. If you are one who can listen, she will sing for you her song of celebration.

A blend of animal and man? Promises and celebration? Whose song did she sing? Seeking understanding, I returned to Earth Visions the next day. Three young women were admiring the Deer Maiden. "I love her!" exclaimed one. "She is beautiful."

I looked around the spacious pastel room. Gorgeous crystals of every shape and color bore testimony to God's creative artistry—and to the human craving for empowerment. But when I glimpsed the painting across from me—a lovely woman gazing into a lake and seeing her image reflected as a wolf—I prayed for guidance. Moments later, sensing God's protection and confirmation, I began to examine the bookshelves. Joseph Campbell's *The Power of Myth* caught my eye. I opened it and read:

> What is a myth? The dictionary definition of a myth would be stories about gods.... What is a god? A god is a personification of a motivating power or value system that functions in human life and in the universe—the powers of your own body and of nature. The myths are metaphorical of spiritual potentiality in the human being, and the same powers that animate our life animate the life of the world...
>
> We need myths that will identify the individual not with his local group but with his planet.[3]

Myths as a Guiding Force.

Webster defines *myth* as a "traditional story or legend... concerning supernatural beings... often serving to explain natural phenomena or the origins of a people."[4] To primitive people, myths served as their basic body of truth. These myths shaped and sustained their culture. Contemporary myths which influence our culture today may not include supernatural beings or the occult. But if they are based on wrong premises, pseudo-science, or false hopes, they will breed defeat, disharmony, and disillusionment.

God wants to shape and sustain our culture with truth. That means that we need to know and follow His wisdom (including the whole body of scientific or natural facts which He designed), not "turn aside to myths" (2 *Timothy* 4:4).

Since pagan societies sought secret wisdom through magic and spiritism, they drew inspiration from the same occult source. It is not surprising that many myths from around the world simulate biblical history and resemble one another. Satan's army of demons, hiding behind the diverse masks of man-made deities,[5] happily supplied pagan priests with counterfeit versions of God's revealed truth. Thus, man-made myths blended occult revelations with human imagination. Notice how this is happening all around us today.

Why are myths so important to Deep Ecology? Because, explains Thomas Berry in *The Dream of the Earth,* myths and their symbols "provide not only the understanding and the sense of direction that we need, they also evoke the energy . . . "[6] "The traditional story is dysfunctional . . . We need a story that will educate us . . . heal, guide, and discipline us."[7]

The "traditional story" from the Bible denounces paganism as a cruel counterfeit of God's promises. No wonder Deep Ecologists despise "the powerful myth of fundamentalists" and are determined to replace it with one that matches their visions.

Presently we are entering another historical period . . . the ecological age . . . an indication of the interdependence of all living and nonliving systems of the earth. . . . These transformations require the assistance of the entire planet . . . not merely adaption to a reduced supply of fuels. . . . What is happening is something of a far greater magnitude. It is a radical change in our mode of consciousness. Our challenge is to create a new language, even a new sense of what it is to be human.[8] (Thomas Berry)

Now, say Deep Ecologists, it's up to the human species to reverse the process by *creating a new picture of reality*—one more powerful than the obsolete but tenacious myth of Christianity.

Should we rewrite reality?

I heard an alarming bit of myth-making last fall at a teachers' workshop on global education. Demonstrating a lesson in world cultures, the master teacher asked, "Are you familiar with the story about Israel's sudden departure from Egypt?"

Many heads nodded.

"But have you heard the other side? [Pause] The Jews had become so obnoxious that the Pharaoh had to get rid of them. So he sent his army to chase them out."

After the workshop, I asked the instructor where he found that interesting bit of information. He laughed. "I just made it up," he answered, as if rewriting history made perfect sense.

Myth-making makes sense to those who would save the earth by slandering Christianity and reviving pantheism— the belief that the divine life force is in everything. The objective is to communicate mystical myths and pagan powers in contemporary and pleasing terms, so that even children will accept them. Therefore, they will usually contain a measure of truth—enough to sound right. But distorted truth is always a lie—a deception that fits the plan of "the father of lies," Satan himself *(John 8:44)*.

These myths may change to fit the "politically correct" thinking of the day. For example, some years ago, children were taught that the pilgrims thanked the Indians, not God, for their first successful harvest.[9] The following 1990 version of the Thanksgiving myth was circulated to about half of all our nation's elementary schools by *Scholastic News*:

GIVE THANKS TO THE EARTH
The first Thanksgiving feasts were harvest festivals. People gathered to celebrate successful harvests and to *thank the Earth* for its fruits. You can celebrate the earth every day by always taking care of the environment.[10] (emphasis added)

Myths That Transform.

"The Earth is our Mother, we must take care of her. Ha-yonna, Ho-yonna, Ha-nana..." The fourth-graders happily chanted the repetitive words along with the teacher. Some shook Indian rattles. Others drummed out the beat with elderberry clacking sticks. "I am the forest, I am the trees... Ha-yonna, ho-yanna." It was fun. A few Girl Scouts already knew the song and accompanying movements.

What did the strange words mean?

"Something about giving power," explained the teacher.

Moments later, the children learned to play Native American games. Two teams took turns throwing Indian dice (painted black walnut halves filled with pitch). The team throwing the dice chanted to invoke the helpful presence of "good spirits." The opposing team tapped the ground, inviting interference from "distracting spirits."

Did the spirits accept the invitation? Maybe. Together, pagan beliefs and repetitive chants can awaken occult power. Yet, contrary to popular myths—demonic forces will not necessarily be manipulated by human formulas. Remember, "the whole world is under the control of the evil one" (1 John 5:19), not subject to incantations of magicians.

There is nothing wrong with learning about mythology. Earth-centered myths can provide valuable insights into world cultures. But when schools replace facts with fantasy and emphasize subjective experience rather than objective knowledge, they produce cultural illiterates—children who will believe anything. When myths are presented to students who have not built a mental framework based on a historical perspective, and when these mythical beliefs are reinforced with "fun" pagan practices, they can serve as alluring bait for occult spirituality.

This is happening today. While factual knowledge is diminishing in the classroom, myths are fast multiplying. Look at these examples:

☐ Each book in a classroom ecology series opens with a full-page picture of a god or goddess—one that could be copied and used to "make attractive covers" for the students' personalized notebooks. *Floods and Droughts*, begins with a look at the fierce-looking Chinese weather god, Lei Chen Tzu. Along with useful facts on climate, the book introduces flood myths from around the world and tells the student to write his "own Indian legend."[11]

□ *Natural Wonders,* a creative play book for kindergarten and preschool, suggests a Rain Dance as part of its demonstration of how rain forms—a typical example of myth riding on the back of solid, helpful facts. After introducing the myth ("If they danced and chanted to the gods of nature, rain would pour . . ."), the book presented two activities, one good, one deceptive.

> Put about one inch of hot water in a large jar and put a metal pan of ice cubes on top. Then place the jar carefully in a dark place and use a flashlight to look for the cloud. Keep watching to see the tiny raindrops gather and fall to the bottom.

> *Do a rain dance and enjoy the gift from the nature gods![12]*

□ Among the best-read books in nationwide school and public libraries are the scary, mystical stories that blur the line between reality and fantasy, and, like pagan myths, breathe supernatural ideas into everyday existence. Yes, they differentiate between good and evil characters, but both sides use occult formulas to manipulate "cosmic" forces. Ponder the last two sentences in this statement from the brochure for the Literature Docent Program in our local Los Altos Schools:

> Mythical beings and stories were once alive in the same way that all ideas are alive as long as they are believed. *Beliefs, more than facts, influence man's fears, dreams and actions. . . . Through myths, man faithfully searches for light in dark places.*

Beyond Reality.

A cheery little book from the Midwest titled *Twelve* guides teachers and students alike on an enticing search for "light in dark places." Like many other fantasies based on the myth of spiritual oneness, it makes the darkness seem bright indeed. Dedicated to Madeleine L'Engle, Isaac Asimov, Carl Sagan, and the "Caretakers of Mankind," it first found a place in special education and is now spreading into programs for gifted children.

Author Elaine Kittredge, a kind sincere mother who told me that she trusts God, believes in all religions, and follows her inner voice, wrote a fantasy about preteen Jimmy who enters a dreamlike state one moonlit night to the sound of faraway music. He floats through the air, slides through a spectrum of colors, soars to the stars, and meets a happy elf who blends with the plants and teaches Jimmy telepathic communication through *mental projection*—"*focus* all my thoughts into a point and shoot it to him."[13]

Soon Jimmy can alter his consciousness at will and enjoy his unity with other species. He moves back and forth between the ordinary world and that dreamy realm where trees talk, stars sing, faeries explain psychic seeing, and all the plants have their own spirit entities called *devas*. Since trees become his best friends, Jimmy sobs at the sight of a log burning in the fireplace. After all, the "trees on the planet hold it together [by] pulling energy from the sky and putting it into the ground with their roots."[14]

The book's endorsements suggest an amazing acceptance of occult adventure: "A wonderful book for the young and the old . . . " says Gerald Jampolsky, M.D., author of *Love Is Letting Go of Fear*. "I hope it will have all the success it deserves," adds Madeleine L'Engle. "A lovely, sensitive tale of a child's awareness of two realities," agrees Michael Harner, author of *The Way of the Shaman*.

When mythical images emphasize environmental goals and universal oneness, they become all the more appealing. Just look again at Jimmy. Could children identify with his commission? Would they want to come along on his journey? Those who imitate his occult formulas may experience an *illusion* of a spiritual reality that usually appears beautiful for a season—before the oppression begins.

The tree was moving gently behind my back. I could feel the water seeping up slightly underneath the bark.

The bark felt like the skin of big quiet animal...
"Jimmy!"
"Yes, I'm Jimmy."
"You have been chosen to be a tree and plant friend.
Your job is to find a way to bring humans back to tree
entities so that we may share our wisdom and love of
the planet. We don't have a lot of time, Jimmy. Can
you work with us?"[15]

Jimmy's story provides exactly what deep ecologists and
ecotheologians seek: A "new story" that will counter the
dualistic beliefs that separate fantasy from reality and paganism from truth. But other kinds of stories also accomplish this goal. "Tales of mythological gods and their involvement with men are not far removed from modern-day
science fiction stories of encounters with alien beings on far
planets,"[16] writes Michael Banks in *Understanding Science
Fiction.*

Banks is right. Both pagan myths and science fiction
cause us to imagine a world that doesn't exist. The insights
and images of science fiction can benefit those readers who
draw a clear line between reality and fiction. But when
science fiction (like myths) become, as Banks recommends,
"useful as [science] course supplements,"[17] there is need for
caution. Unless children are equipped to resist, the mystical/
mythical delights students feast on these days will strip
them of the very tools that could help them make wise
evaluations: factual knowledge and a clear view of reality.

Never before have I seen such a direct, purposeful and
successful attempt at destroying the rational thinking of children as there is today. Strangely enough, this destruction is
coming through the very institutions in which we have placed
our greatest trust—our educational system.[18] (Richard B. Bliss,
Ed.D.)

WHAT CAN FAMILIES DO?

☐ Affirm the truths of the Armor of God daily (see chap. 2).
☐ Understand and discuss . . .
1. The difference between truth and myth.
2. God's plan for the care of His creation.
3. God's intended relationship between humans and animals.
4. The use of facts to identify myths.
☐ Chose a family project from pages 170–175.

1. THE DIFFERENCE BETWEEN BIBLICAL TRUTH AND PAGAN MYTH. Most of those who wrote the truths of the Bible were eyewitnesses to the events they described (2 *Peter 1:16*). They heard God's voice, saw His miracles, followed His guidelines, acted by the power of His Spirit, and experienced His triumph. The prophecies they communicated came true—miraculously, amazingly, consistently. That Isaiah 53 foretold Christ's crucifixion in detail 700 years before it happened has baffled His opponents and caused countless attempts to shuffle, divide, and redate Old Testament books.

In contrast, false prophets claim to hear and see divine manifestations, but the fruit of their lives exposes the source of their revelation. God's prophecies spoken through His servants *always* come true. False prophets can boast no such record (*Deuteronomy 18:22*).

Myths don't claim to be true; therefore, they escape rational scrutiny. Their power to persuade comes not from reliability but from desirability. The promiscuous and violent gods and goddesses in pagan myths model a lifestyle that matches nature's cravings and models the lie: sin is fun; therefore, it is good.

Today, as back in Old and New Testament days, myths which oppose God's truth are endowed with power to teach us about ourselves and the earth. That's why Deep Ecologists promote them. Paul's warning fits our times: "Have nothing to do with godless myths" (*1 Timothy 4:7*). Instead, know truth!

Discuss these passages: Isaiah 5:20; 1 Timothy 1:3-7, 4:7; 2 Timothy 4:3-4; 2 Peter 1:16.

2. GOD'S PLAN FOR THE CARE OF HIS CREATION. God's prescription for a healthy earth opposes pagan myths and pantheistic beliefs on every point. First, He made people, not animals, in His image, so that our actions would reflect His divine love. (See *Galatians 2:20; Genesis 1:26-27*.) Second, He wants us to guard the earth according to *His* wisdom, not the spirit of Gaia. He told us, "Fill the earth

Chart 3: TRUTHS THAT COUNTER MYTHS	
© 1992 Berit Kjos	
CONTEMPORARY MYTHS	*TRUTHS THAT COUNTER THE LIES*
Prehistoric cultures, led by Mother Goddess, enjoyed perfect harmony	The Lord saw how great man's wickedness on earth had become . . . Gen. 6:5
Male god(s) brought war, exploitation	In Him all things hold together. Col. 1:17
A spiritual evolution will save the earth and restore peace and harmony	The Sovereign Lord says . . . "I will create . . . a new earth." Isa. 65:17; Rev. 21:1
Children must be socialized (conformed to society's values and practices)	Do not conform any longer to the pattern of this world . . . Rom. 12:2
Rewrite earth's story based on wisdom from primal societies	The wisdom of this world is foolishness in God's sight. 1 Cor. 3:19

and subdue it. . . . I give you every seed-bearing plant on the face of the whole earth and every tree that has fruit with seed in it. They will be yours for food" *(Genesis 1:28-29)*. To Noah, God said, "Everything that lives and moves will be food for you" *(Genesis 9:3)*. But there was a condition added to the provision. God's command—to "subdue" and "rule" the earth and its creatures—implied caring responsibility, not license to pollute and misuse. Our Creator intended to demonstrate His compassionate character through us, not give free reign to an undisciplined animal like nature in us.

> The "image of God" in which man was created must entail those aspects of human nature which are not shared by animals—attributes such as moral consciousness, the ability to think abstractly, an understanding of beauty and emotion, and above all, the capacity for worshiping and loving God. This eternal and divine dimension of man's being must be the essence of what is involved in the likeness of God.[19] (Dr. Henry Morris in *Genesis Record*)

Throughout the Bible, God shows us that people are more precious to Him than all the other marvelous parts of His creation. He made us to be His own sons and daughters, friends with whom He could share His heart, disciples who would communicate His eternal purpose, and servants who would carry out His plan here on earth. Listen to what He told His loyal servant and friend, Moses:

> You yourselves have seen what I did to Egypt, and how I carried you on eagles' wings and brought you to Myself. Now if you obey Me fully and keep My covenant, then out of all nations you will be My treasured possession. Although the whole earth is Mine, you will be for Me a kingdom of priests and a holy nation (*Exodus 19:4-6*).

Even before He created the earth, our Father longed to communicate His love and values to His yet-to-be-born people. He wanted us to grow up to be mature in character, trained for responsibility, equipped to care for His family business—the rest of His creation. Looking forward to intimate friendship with adult sons and daughters, He offered us His name, His honor, His riches, and His life.

But from the beginning, His people chose their own ways. As the result, they gradually aligned themselves more with the animals than with the Creator who offered them an intimate and unending love-relationship. "Man was intended to replenish the earth by looking after it," said Oswald Chambers, "[but] sin has made man its tyrant." The Prophet Isaiah understood the tragedy and shared God's sadness.

> I will sing to the one I love a song about his vineyard:
> My loved one had a vineyard on a fertile hillside.
> He dug it up and cleared it of stones and planted it
> with the choicest of vines. . . . Then he looked for a
> crop of good grapes, but it yielded only bad fruit.
>
> Now I will tell you what I am going to do to my
> vineyard. I will make it a wasteland, neither pruned
> nor cultivated, and briers and thorns will grow there. I
> will command the clouds not to rain on it *(Isaiah 5:1-6)*.

We are His vineyard. We are also His stewards—the guardians of His trees, flowers, rivers, and animals. If we are willing to follow truth, He will bless the land and show us how to care for it.

Discuss these passages: Genesis 1:28-30, 2:8, 9:3; Proverbs 12:10; 1 Corinthians 10:23-26, 31.

3. GOD'S INTENDED RELATIONSHIP BETWEEN HUMANS AND ANIMALS. Granting certain rights to animals, God said, "And to all the beasts of the earth and all the birds of the air and all the creatures that move on the ground—everything that has the breath of life in it—I give every green plant for food" *(Genesis 1:30)*.

While God makes a clear distinction between humans and animals, we live together in this world. He wants us to care for His creatures. We may also use them—according to His kind wisdom. "Are not two sparrows sold for a penny?" asks Jesus. "Yet not one of them will fall to the ground apart from the will of your Father. . . . So don't be afraid; you are worth more than many sparrows" *(Matthew 10:29, 31)*.

Since God cares for sparrows, so should we. But how? The dilemmas of stewardship challenge us to continually hear and heed the mind of the Creator. What did He mean when He said: "Everything that lives and moves will be food for you ... And to all the beasts of the earth ... I give every green plant for food"? *(Genesis 9:3; 1:30)*

The questions surrounding man's responsibilities to animals are complex and controversial. Myths that teach the sanctity of the wolf suggest that wolves must be allowed to multiply freely. But should they be given freedom to multiply near Wyoming's ranches where they feed on domestic sheep, at a great loss to local farmers? Should Montana farmers be allowed to shoot diseased and contagious bison who wander into their flocks and infect grazing cattle? Who has first rights to the Oregon forests—the endangered spotted owl or the thousands of employees whose jobs depend on the logging industry?

To the animal-rights activists who have traded truth for myth, kindness is not enough. As Tim Stafford reported in *Christianity Today:*

> Today, the most visible animal-rights activists speak out against the belief that humankind has been put in charge of creation. This presumption, they claim, has led to the overwhelming slavery and abuse that animals suffer. They scoff at the Christian requirement that we treat animals kindly. It is, they say, like the requirement that slaveowners treat their slaves kindly. The activist's goal is to set the animals free—free from all human control and domination.[20]

Medical research is no excuse. "I don't believe it is morally permissible to exploit weaker beings, even if we derive benefits,"[21] says law professor Gary Francione.

Even if a pig's heart could save a human baby's life? When this question was raised in a *Harper's* forum on the morality of animal experimentation, one animal-rights activist demanded that the baby's mother must be taught to show concern for the pig.

This position makes sense to those who reverse God's

order, placing animals on a spiritual pedestal. They argue that Earth has more than enough humans but far too few spotted owls and wolves to balance its psychic energies. The human animal, they say, is the least desirable and most dispensable of Earth's species.

That argument pales in the light of truth. For example, when Israel settled in the Promised Land, God told His people that He would not drive out all the pagan inhabitants immediately "because the land would become desolate and the wild animals too numerous for you." In other words, God would maintain a human population large enough to keep predators from invading human territories, not vice versa *(Exodus 23:29)*.

God sets boundaries for animals and us. His kindness reaches out to *all* His creatures. To help us treat them as He would, He has instructed us to . . .

☐ Share food with wild animals, Exodus 23:10-11.
☐ Give domestic animals time to rest, Exodus 23:12.
☐ Protect wild birds, Deuteronomy 22:6.
☐ Don't burden livestock unfairly, Deuteronomy 22:10.
☐ Share grain with livestock, Deuteronomy 25:4.

In an ideal agricultural setting, humans and domestic animals work together and fit into each others' lives in both personal and practical ways. Thus, a sheep may be a much-loved pet as well as future food and clothing.

In a more artificial setting, we can easily view God's creatures from a narrow, self-centered perspective. I recall one day blurting out a wishful, thoughtless kind of statement like, "I would love to have a pet lamb." My boys heard it, did some research, found a sheep farm, and *almost* bought me a live lamb for Mother's Day. At the last moment (God must have nudged them), they decided to make sure I *really* did want a lamb that would transform into a sheep.

We discussed the probable needs of a lamb/sheep and *my* responsibilities as its shepherdess. "Would it be fair," I asked, "to bring it here just to satisfy my whimsical desire to love a lamb and to experience all the wonderful spiritual truths shepherd-author Phillip Keller communicates in his books?" We agreed it was not. My sons decided to settle for a low maintenance toy lamb.

> To gaze upward and think oneself divine is sinful pride; to gaze downward and think oneself no more than plant or animal results in sinful degradation. One is the error common to the New Age Movement; the other is the error common to evolutionism.[22] (Dean A. Ohlman, founder of *Christian Nature Federation*)

4. THE USE OF FACTS TO IDENTIFY MYTHS. Since environmental literature tends to encourage students to imitate the beliefs and lifestyles of primitive people, we need to recognize the underlying myths. Behind the beautiful side of paganism—the illusions of oneness, lie the same human tendencies that bring pain and destruction to all parts of the world: greed, violence, competition, and war.

The late Dr. Clark Wissler, Curator Emeritus of the Department of Anthropology at the American Museum of Natural History, was recognized as a world authority on Native Americans. In *Indians of the United States*, he describes all the admirable aspects of their culture: their love for their children, their hospitality, their belief in the power of the peace pipe to establish bonds of friendship.

Then, exposing the sad facts along with the good, Dr. Wissler strips away the popular myth of perfect harmony. In the end, we see that Native Americans struggle with the same human nature we do. Look at the popular myths in the light of additional facts:

☐ Harmony with nature? To stampede a herd of buffalo, hunters might set the grass on fire behind the flock. The escaping herd would "flounder into a swamp or tumble over a cliff."[23] "Near Folsom, New Mexico, in 1926 excavators uncovered the skeletons of a small herd of the now extinct *Bison taylori*. . . . Most tail bones were missing, hinting at the world of human hands that cut away the tails with the skins."[24]

☐ Preserver of life? "The early Indian hunted the wild horse for food, which may be one of the reasons why they became extinct long before white men came to America."[25]

☐ Peace with each other? "The elders of neighboring tribes talked peace and at times sincerely sought it, but the marauding traditions were so carefully fostered that raiding for blood, captives, and plunder was on the level of second nature." "Great social acclaim went to the man returning with both scalps and horses."[26]

☐ Respect for all life? The Iroquois, noted for democratic self-government, "now planned to destroy the Huron. It was not to be a war of subjugation; they hated the Huron intensely, like brother against brother. After taking the first town, they massacred its entire population. . . . It is believed that more than 10,000 Huron were killed."[27]

☐ Destroyed by white man's aggression? The Iroquois destroyed other tribes, "only at last to waste away itself in an effort to conrol the Algonquin. It was not the white man who destroyed the Iroquois Family, though he dealt harshly with a few surviving remnants, but a case of brother against brother. . . . "[28]

I don't want to diminish the wrongs committed against Native Americans: killing, introducing new diseases, selling alcohol, taking their land, ignoring treaty obligations. . . . Yet our children need to see these tragic violations in the light of the whole truth. Apart from our Creator and Shepherd, human nature everywhere will express its selfishness and violence. To dismiss uncomfortable facts in order to prove a *false ideal* perpetuates the lies. It also hides the only solution that works—knowing and trusting God.

> There is no faithfulness, no love, no acknowledgement of God in the land. There is only cursing, lying and murder, stealing and adultery. . . . Because of this the land mourns, and all who live in it waste away; the beasts of the field and the birds of the air and the fish of the sea are dying . . . my people are destroyed from lack of knowledge . . .
> Come let us return to the Lord *(Hosea 4:1-3, 6; 6:1).*

Witchcraft and Ecology

The model of the Goddess ... fosters respect for the sacredness of all living things. Witchcraft can be seen as a religion of ecology. Its goal is harmony with nature, so that life may not just survive, but thrive.
—Starhawk, first president of the Covenant of the Goddess[1]

The human woman gives birth just as the earth gives birth to the plants ... so woman magic and earth magic are the same.
—Joseph Campbell[2]

He turned rivers into a desert, flowing springs into thirsty ground, and fruitful land into a salt waste, because of the wickedness of those who lived there. (Psalm 107:33-34)

TIM, AN EIGHTH-GRADER at a Christian middle school, walked into the home of a close friend and sensed that something had changed. It felt spooky. What was wrong?

"My sister has become a witch," explained his friend.

That wasn't all. Her boyfriend was the warlock leader of a growing coven of witches.

Tim was ready for the challenge. He told his friend about spiritual warfare, and then prayed for his protection and for freedom for his sister. Tim was learning to trust God daily for his own safety from the hostile advances of the coven members who gathered near his own home.

"They cast spells on kids they don't like," he told me a week later. "One boy fell and broke his arm."

Tim's experience is being duplicated across the nation. For the young, witchcraft may be the fastest growing form of occult empowerment. Masquerading as environmental spirituality, it provides a noble cause as well as the promise of secret power. A friend of my son described some strange happenings at his high school:

> Some kids in my school are environmentalists and are totally for taking care of the earth and saving the animals. They believe in world peace and make the peace sign with their fingers. "We should combine everybody and make one world," they say.
>
> Today they got into a circle around a cross they formed with little white chips. They read from a black book and held each other's pinkies. Then they closed their eyes, leaned their heads way back, and talked in a weird language. Afterwards I asked them, "What were you guys doing in there?"
>
> "We're practicing our witchcraft," they answered.
>
> In the world religions class, they study Buddhism. Sometimes the teacher puts on eerie music. They all lie down on the floor and chant to themselves. They have rituals and weird stuff like inner body feelings.
>
> One guy told me the meditations are great. "I get into trance and it's really weird. I can't even describe it."
>
> I told him that he could get demon-possessed. That really freaked him out. He said, "Why didn't you tell me earlier?"

Loving Nature.

Chants, trance, ritual, and power.... Add nature, and you have a spiritual medley that is captivating adults as well as teenagers throughout the Western World. Like the New Age movement, witchcraft is influencing our culture far beyond the borders of its countless covens (independent local groups).

Starhawk, priestess of the Old Religion of the Goddess, is one of the craft's leading ambassadors. An instructor at Matthew Fox's Institute for Culture and Creation, she and others who share her pagan persuasions have been teaching wiccan rituals and the "positive" side of witchcraft in church groups and seminaries[3] across the country—sometimes leaving a storm of protest in their wake.

"Witchcraft is ... perhaps the oldest religion existent in the West," writes Starhawk in *The Spiral Dance,* a manual on witchcraft which is also used in Women's Studies in colleges, universities—and even in some seminaries.

> The Old Religion, as we call it, is closer in spirit to Native American traditions or to the shamanism of the Arctic. Witchcraft takes its teachings from nature, and reads inspiration in the movements of the sun, moon, and stars, the flight of birds, the slow growth of trees, and the cycles of the seasons.[4]

Zealous protectors of the environment, witches view the earth as the physical manifestation of the Goddess. To them, the earth is the sacred body of the goddess, whose lifeforce flows through everything. Like deep ecologists, they seek a spiritual transformation of our culture.

"Many of us who are trying to reconnect with the land are realizing that what is needed is a regeneration of culture," wrote Judith Plant in *Healing the Wounds.* "What we are seeking is a religion that connects us to the land. Many of us ... try to emulate the native people."[5]

Not only do neopagans—a euphemism for sorcerers, witches, and other followers of the Goddess—care about the earth, but they also know how to invoke her power to "do magic." In a televised dialogue on "Hard Copy," two coven members shared their views of witchcraft, its practices, and their love for the earth. In the background, a circle of witches chanted, "We call on you to enter in ... "

> *Moderator:* Felicity and Ruth seem ordinary enough, they have families, jobs, nice homes—if you had just met them on the street you probably wouldn't even realize that they are practicing witches. Felicity rules the wind. Ruth plans to bring about the downfall of male dominance ...

> *Ruth:* There are attorneys that are witches, insurance

salespeople, all kinds of scientists, and medical doctors.

Moderator: They don't burn witches any more—but they are still under fire. But they are coming out of the broom closet by the coven to let the world know that there is a good side to witchcraft and that they are anything but Satan worshipers...

Felicity: The religion of witchcraft is a religion about life, the preservation of life, the worship of life, the reverence and respect for life...

Moderator: They call themselves healers and practice the same witchcraft that was alive long before Christianity... only their best friends know their secret: that they are feminist witches, heavy into ecology. That they want to save the earth and make it safe for women and children.

Ruth: As witches, we ally ourselves with the forces of nature, and when we invoke the elements, we can, in conjunction with them, create what we want—and that's what casting spells is. It's calling on all the forces of nature and our own power to direct our will in a particular way—to get what we want.[6]

As enthusiastic witches like Ruth and Felicity spread the word, multitudes listen. Many are captivated by the alluring blend of environmental consciousness, spiritual power, and erotic thrills. In 1990, witches in the San Francisco Bay Area allegedly numbered 15,000 to 20,000. Nationwide, the count was 150,000 to 175,000 and growing fast, according to the *Bay Area Pagan Assemblies* (BAPA), an umbrella organization for witches, druids, shamans, and followers of Goddess spirituality, "formed to fight Christian resistance to New Age practices."[7]

Although witchcraft opposes the Church, many Christians are embracing it. A graduate student at the School of Theology at Claremont completed a class titled "Religious Education Curriculum Design" by planning a curriculum for women who had become disillusioned with "the traditional patriarchal church."[8] She based her curriculum on contemporary witchcraft—specifically rituals from Starhawk's book *The Spiral Dance*. When she presented her plan to the class, her professor and fellow trainees for Christian ministry responded not with shock but with appreciation for "a wonderful idea."[9]

Promotion of witchcraft in public schools, colleges, television, and movies has stirred curiosity and fascination. Who wouldn't want to manipulate the force when it is offered in the name of self-empowerment of preservation of the earth? Nobody warns the seeker that witchcraft is abhorrent to God, destructive to our land, and potentially deadly to the naive experimenter.

> Pagan rituals . . . involve concentrating upon a single thought or intention. Instead of a petition to God to make something happen, pagans try to focus the Goddess energy within themselves and their surroundings, and become a channel for that energy. Spells and rituals are ways of centering and focusing much the same as Buddhist chanting . . . [10] (Phyllis Evelyn Johnson)

Practicing Mind Control.

Celtic witchcraft, the "Lady of the Light," and the force of "the Dark" battle for dominance in a children's book called *The Dark Is Rising*—required reading for sixth-graders in a public school in Los Altos, California. To maximize student interest and involvement, the teacher encouraged her class to experiment with the mind-control practices shown in the book: "Just do it for a giggle."

Sarah, a Christian, recognized the occult messages and refused to participate. "I don't want anyone to read my mind," she told her mother. Her mother talked with the teacher who agreed to excuse Sarah from the reading assignment. She later chose a new reader for the whole class.

Did Sarah have reason to fear? Many people—both in and outside the Church—downplay the danger of dabbling in the occult. But neopagans know the power of an exciting story, a creative imagination, and the lure of magic. The Winter 1989 issue of *Sage Woman*, "A Quarterly Magazine of Women's Spirituality," featured "Reading Selections for the Young Pagan." To encourage youngsters in the "craft," book editor Lunaea promoted *The Dark Is Rising* and its four companion books by Susan Cooper:

> This pentology goes back to the deep pagan roots of the Arthurian epic, as modern-day children aid in the struggle between good and evil. I particularly liked *Greenwitch*, the third book in the series, when the female protagonist, Jane, is invited to a special women-only ritual involving the sea. This story is full of mystery, beauty, and deep magic.[11]

I borrowed *The Dark Is Rising* from our local children's library. This Newbery Honor Book tells about a midwinter solstice battle between the occult powers of the good Light and the evil Dark, which forces young Will Stanton to learn the ancient magical ways from the Old Ones. Point by point, the story's symbols, techniques, and rituals match those in Starhawk's witchcraft manual, *The Spiral Dance*.

The chart on page 68 compares the occult practices shown in *The Dark Is Rising* with those in Starhawk's manual.

Notice that the two columns match in concept but differ in content: *The Spiral Dance* presents the teaching and *The Dark Is Rising* shows how it works.

Like Israel during the time of the Judges, our nation seems to be rapidly turning from God to flagrant paganism. When my oldest son attended Sarah's elementary school a few years earlier, he learned academics in an environment guarded from occult influences by the presence of the Holy Spirit in a Christian principal and two Christian teachers. After they retired, earthy spirituality swept into the classrooms.

"We have all this power we don't even know we have," exclaimed the current fifth-grade teacher to her class. Wide-eyed, her students listened as she described the events of a

Chart 4: FORMULAS FOR MIND CONTROL

© 1992 Berit Kjos

THE SPIRAL DANCE[12]	THE DARK IS RISING[13]
WORKING MAGIC THROUGH MIND CONTROL	
Of all the disciplines of magic, the art of moving energy is the . . . most natural . . . *Picture* the power in motion, and it moves. *Feel* it flowing and it flows . . .	Will *thought hard*, in furious concentration, *of the image* of the blazing blazing log fire . . . He *felt* the warmth . . . "Go out, fire," he said to it in his mind . . . "Go out." And the fire went out.
SYMBOLS: CHANNELS OF POWER	
The *quartered circle* is basic to Witchcraft . . . the physical objects we use in Witchcraft, are the *tangible representatives of unseen forces.* Power, the subtle force that shapes reality, is raised through chanting or dancing and may be *directed through a symbol or visualization.*	He felt from the Signs (quartered circles) a fierce sensation . . . a strong, arrogant reassurance of power. Will filled his whole mind with the picture of the great circle of tall candle-flames . . . he *struck forward in his mind with the column of light.*
CASTING SPELLS	
To cast a spell is to project energy through a symbol . . . Spells . . . require the combined faculties of relaxation, visualization, concentration, and projection.	Under that spell I have your sister bound by totem magic . . . A birth sign and a hair of the head are excellent totems.
ALTERED CONSCIOUSNESS: THE DOOR TO OCCULT SPIRITUALITY	
Expanded awareness begins with dreams. . . . "the *Door* of Dreams."	The *doors* are our great *gateway into Time,* you will know more about the uses of them before long.
THE GREAT GODDESS: SOURCE OF WISDOM, POWER, AND LIFE	
The Goddess continually offers us challenges, but knowing that *she is within us as well as around us,* we find the strength to meet them.	This silent *music that entered Will's mind* and took hold of his spirit came . . . *from the old Lady.* Without speech, she was speaking to him.
A MALE GOD (THE HORNED SATAN) RANKS BELOW THE GODDESS	
The *Horned God* . . . wears horns— but they are the waxing and waning crescents of the Goddess Moon, and the symbol of *animal vitality* . . .	*The [Hunter's head] was horned* with the antlers of a stag. . . . Will saw the cruelty now as the *fierce inevitability of nature.*

Mind-Control Workshop she had enjoyed with the new principal and another teacher. After a series of mental exercises, the three educators had joined hundreds of other participants in walking barefoot across red-hot coals to prove their newfound power. The ancient ritual (practiced as early as 500 B.C. in China, Japan, Tibet, and India) seemed simple enough: raise hands, clench fists, chant about cool moss, and visualize its soothing softness underfoot.

"Doing magic" through imaging, chanting, ritual celebrations, and altered consciousness can produce captivating results: dramatic mind-over-body feats, an intoxicating sense of empowerment, heightened self-esteem, and an illusion of interconnectedness with "Mother Earth and her spirits." But at what cost? Like Pinnochio's donkey-eared playmates on Treasure Island, gullible seekers pay for Satan's enticing favors with their freedom and their lives.

Magic is the craft of Witchcraft . . . to weave the unseen forces into form . . . to leap beyond imagination into that space between the worlds where fantasy becomes real; to be at once animal and god.[14] (Starhawk)

Witches may or may not believe in nature spirits. They usually don't believe that their magic could be empowered by an evil force. To them, the powers they manipulate are merely part of a morally neutral nature—the Great Goddess.

Yet, they contradict their own doctrines. Though most modern witches view the Goddess force as neither good nor evil, they would probably tell you that *white* magic is neutral or good, while *black* magic is evil. In other words, the *intent* determines the value.

The Bible shows that the *source* of supernatural power determines its value. Does it flow from God or Satan? No matter how beneficial the power may seem, if it springs from the latter, it opposes God's purpose and accomplishes evil. Remember Deuteronomy 18:9-11, "Let no one be found among you who . . . practices divination or sorcery, interprets omens, engages in witchcraft, or casts spells."

Since witches draw wisdom as well as power from the demonic forces behind the Goddess, their beliefs are full of twisted truths and captivating contradictions. Their name stems from the old Anglo-Saxon word *wicce* which means "bend or shape," and, indeed, witches try to *bend* reality and shape the unseen according to their will to fit their demands. However, many contemporary witches claim that *wicce* means "wise," which also fits. Demonstrating the folly of "serving created things rather than the Creator," they illustrate the truth of Romans 1: "Although they claimed to be wise, they became fools. . . . Therefore God gave them over in the sinful desires of their hearts to sexual impurity" (vv. 22-25).

To neopagans, the physical is as much part of the Goddess force as is the psychic. So why not abandon oneself to all kinds of physical pleasure? As Starhawk has said, "Union with the Goddess comes through embracing the material world. In witchcraft, we do not fight self-interest; we follow it, but with an awareness that transmutes it into something sacred."[15]

Sacred self-interest? This contradiction is seducing a public that is panting for excuses to engage in mystical, sensual thrills that will enlighten and empower the self. And when this lie is joined to the hope of healing the earth, it snares multitudes. In an article written for the *Christian Research Journal*, Craig Hawkins explains this twisted view of good and evil:

> Sin is viewed as an outdated concept that is "only a tool used to shackle the minds and actions of people." The only "sin" or evil is that of being unbalanced and out of harmony or estranged from oneself, others, the varied life forms, and Mother Earth. As there is no sin or divine retribution to be saved from, "salvation" has only to do with attaining and maintaining harmony with the above.[16]

God has shown us that witchcraft, sorcery, magic, and sexual promiscuity breed addiction to those behaviors, separation from God, and spiritual death. Terrible bondage occurs, not because God inflicts it, but because the victims—having rejected God's protective love—bring it on themselves. In spite of popular illusions about nature's goodness, human nature tends to be self-centered rather than self-giving. Under the guidance and power of demonic spirits, it eventually becomes capricious, hateful, cruel, and deadly.

Craig Hawkins describes this misguided belief system and the source of the force: "Despite what witches claim, witchcraft originates from Satan—the 'father of lies' and the 'god of this world,' and from man's corrupt nature. Thus, though witches do not acknowledge the Devil's existence, they are nontheless (all the more so) trapped in the talons of his tyrannical grip."[17]

WHAT CAN FAMILIES DO?

☐ Continue to affirm the truth outlined in the Armor.
☐ Know and discuss . . .
 1. The Scriptures that deal with witchcraft.
 2. The underlying reason for earth's problems.
☐ Choose a family project from pages 170–175.

1. THE SCRIPTURES THAT DEAL WITH WITCHCRAFT:
☐ Know why you need to avoid witchcraft: Deuteronomy 18:9-11; 1 Samuel 15:23; Galatians 5:19-25.
☐ Know why Old Testament warnings and promises apply to us today: Matthew 5:17-20 and 1 Corinthians 10:1-13.
☐ As Galatians 5:16-20 points out, witchcraft fits right into the basic desires of our human nature. Study the rest of Galatians 5, and discuss the differences between "sinful nature" (the flesh) and God's Spirit.
☐ In order to resist witchcraft, you need to know how to recognize it. Review Chart 4. Notice Starhawk's basic formula for spellcasting: a combination of *relaxation, visualization, concentration* (or focus), and mental *projection*. Starhawk's use of the first three is a counterfeit of God's good gifts. The last—a willful manipulation of psychic forces—has no Christian counterpart. Remember, God leads

us, we don't manipulate Him (*Acts 17:24-26*). But human nature has always sought ways to rebel against God and manipulate the forces of nature.

After looking at the chart, turn your mind to God. Sing a praise song or read a psalm. Then thank Him for keeping you safe.

2. THE UNDERLYING REASON FOR EARTH'S PROBLEMS. Back in the early sixties, my husband and I visited Petra, the "pink city" dramatized in the movie, *Indiana Jones and the Last Crusade*. The trip to Edom's ancient capital began in Amman, Jordan, with a four-hour drive south through the desert. Only an occasional camel train or bedouin tent interrupted the sandy, stony barrenness. Finally, at the mountainous entrance to Petra, the passage once blocked to Moses and his followers, we mounted horses and rode through a narrow gorge.

Near the end of the stony corridor the view grew spectacular. The vertical rock walls at our sides framed a sliver of the "pink palace," permitting a teasing glimpse of the rose-colored columns and sculptured ornaments of a palatial wall. What an oasis!

But when we reached the once-flourishing city, the stark sunlight exposed the faded facades of a lifeless ghost town. Behind the broken ruins of a lost civilization hid empty caves—the stripped tombs of a people who long ago separated themselves from God.

Why be surprised? God had told us what to expect. "Edom's streams will be turned into pitch, her dust into burning sulphur," He prophesied long before it happened.

> From generation to generation it will lie desolate . . . God will stretch out over Edom the measuring line of chaos and the plumb line of desolation . . . All her princes will vanish away. Thorns will overrun her citadels, nettles and brambles her strongholds. She will become a haunt for jackals, a home for owls (*Isaiah 34:10-13*).

Talk about climate change! This calamity wasn't caused by chlorofluorocarbons, a hole in the ozone layer, or overpopulation, but because the Edomites dared disobey the King of Kings. Smug and secure in their mountain hideout, they despised Israel and ignored God's covenant. Their arrogant rejection of God's ways and purposes *brought destruction to their land and themselves:*

> This is what the Sovereign LORD says about Edom. . . . "The pride of your heart has deceived you, you who live in the clefts of the rocks and make your home on the heights, you who say to yourself, 'Who can bring me down to the ground?' Though you soar like the eagle and make your nest among the stars, from there I will bring you down" *(Obadiah 1, 3-4).*

Edom literally dried, wilted, and died. Such *desertification* continues to devastate many parts of the world, causing untold suffering from famine and hopelessness. True, humans contribute to desertification by careless farming practices and deforestation. However, Edom's streams and vineyards turned to dust because its people opposed their Maker, and they could do nothing to save their land:

> Edom may say, "Though we have been crushed, we will rebuild the ruins." But this is what the LORD Almighty says: "They may build, but I will demolish. They will be called the Wicked Land, a people always under the wrath of the LORD. You will see it with your own eyes and say, 'Great is the Lord—even beyond the borders of Israel'" *(Malachi 1:4-5).*

Do you wonder how, in today's enlightened, technological world, we can be so naive as to believe that defying God leads to desertification?

Actually, when we prayerfully study Scripture to know God's mind, not to affirm our own views, we discover that the Bible offers sound, unchanging principles that reach far beyond biblical times and the borders of Israel. In 1 Corinthians 10:11, God warns that Old Testament consequences occurred "as examples and were written down as warnings for us, on whom the fulfillment of the ages has come." Now as then, God will bless the land when we obey Him, but He will withhold its resources and bring judgment on the land if we disobey Him.

The Book of Judges shows how decadence can replace faithfulness in less than a generation. When people reject truth as a standard and flirt with seductive spiritual alternatives, the culture crumbles. Hear the grief in God's voice as He watches His people wander away in our pursuit of false gods: "My people have committed two sins: They have forsaken me, the spring of living water, and have dug their own cisterns, broken cisterns that can hold no water" (Jeremiah 2:13).

The broken cisterns were paganism with its seductive gods and goddesses, earthy spirits, and reverence for creation rather than for God. Today they can be Native American shamanism, Balinese trance-spiritism, or plain old witchcraft. It doesn't matter whether they look like pantheism, monism, or polytheism—they all fit together: Pantheism declares that an impersonal god (force, goddess) fills all things, therefore *all is one* (monism) and everything is sacred. Next, humans merely choose their favorite gods (polytheism).

So what does all this have to do with ecology?

In spite of the environmental call for earth-based spirituality, *paganism is not good for the earth*. The goddess of witchcraft brings devastation, not harmony. The power of healing lies in the God's hands alone, so let us heed His warning and do what He says. "If you are willing and obedient, you will eat the best from the land; but if you resist and rebel, you will be devoured .... You will be ashamed because of the sacred oaks in which you have delighted.... You will be like an oak with fading leaves...." (Isaiah 1:19-20, 29-30).

While God hates witchcraft, He loves people and longs to communicate His kindness to the victims of deception. He wants us to be ready with biblical answers and encouragement. For help in counseling someone coming out of occultism, study "How to Live Free from Demonic Oppression" on pages 187–190.

Welcoming the Goddess

Pagans at the Harvard Divinity School. A Goddess-centered ritual at the University of Pennsylvania. A feminist seder in Silver Spring. New moon groups at a rabbinical seminary. Women's spirituality sessions at Appalachian State University, Wesleyan University, Brown....
What on earth is going on?
— Judith Weinraub, *The Washington Post*[1]

In the beginning, there was no God. There was the Goddess. She peered into the great void and created the Heaven and the Earth, and in this new domain women ruled. The world was peaceful and both sexes worshiped Her.
— Sonia L. Nazario, *The Wall Street Journal*[2]

Our Father in heaven, hallowed be Your name, Your kingdom come, Your will be done. (Matthew 6:9-10)

LINDA, A STUDENT in elementary education at California State University at Sacramento, had to take a course titled "Curriculum and Methods in Elementary School Social Studies." On the first day of class, her professor drew a large serpent on the chalkboard. "This will protect you against evil forces," he explained.

"What kind of a class is this?" wondered Linda. A few weeks later, she wrote the following message to her mother who sent it on to me:

> I absolutely hate it! The teacher is wearing a crystal around his neck. If this gives you any idea—here are some of our text titles: *When God Was a Woman, Myths*

to Live By, Return of the Goddess, Cows, Pigs, Wars and Witches, The Once and Future Goddess, etc. If I didn't have to be here, I would have walked out already. I'm so amazed that this is our *required* class.

Linda was being trained to teach Goddess spirituality. As a Christian, she recognized the deception. But what about her peers? What kind of social studies will they be teaching their students? And if the Goddess is spreading her pagan roots through public education, how are her values influencing the rest of the nation?

The Rise of Goddess Spirituality.

During the mid-eighties, I searched local bookstores in vain for information on ancient Canaanite idol worship. I wanted to understand God's prophecy to Abraham concerning the time his descendants would enter the Promised Land. God promised it would happen after 400 years of captivity, when the "sin of the Amorites" reached "its full measure."[3] As always, His timing would be perfect. Israel would not be allowed to possess the land until Canaan's degrading idolatry made it ripe for judgment.

Suddenly, in early 1990, books about Goddess worship burst into public view. With voluptuous illustrations, they described the Babylonian religion that had captivated the Canaanites in earlier days.

Our most popular local bookstore displayed thirty-one books on the Goddess. Some titles, like those on Linda's reading list, express today's growing fascination with the mythical Earth Mother: *The Goddess Returns; The Way of the Goddess—A Manual for Wiccan Initiation; The Serpent and the Goddess—Women, Religions and Power in Celtic Ireland; The Goddess Within; Goddesses in Every Woman; The Sacred Age of the Goddess; The Triple Goddess; The Once and Future Goddess . . .*

Other titles joined Goddess worship to ecofeminism, feminine spirituality, and witchcraft: *Priestesses; Kali-The Feminine Force; The Great Cosmic Mother—Rediscovering the Religions of the Earth; Myth and Sexuality; Drawing Down the Moon—Witches, Druids, Goddess Worshipers and Other Pagans in America Today; The Great Cosmic Mother; The Holy Book of Women's Mysteries—Feminist Witchcraft, Goddess Rituals, Spellcasting and other Womanly Arts.*

Why this outpouring of publicity for the ancient Goddess? Roger Woolger and Jennifer Barker Woolger gave an answer in their article "The Wounded Goddesses Within":

> Throughout the world, but most prominently in Westernized countries, we are witnessing a reawakening of the feminine, a profound upheaval within the consciousness of women. . . . Radical commentators have called it figuratively a "return of the Goddess," because it seems to suggest the very antithesis of patriarchal society.[4]

The myths and practices that beckon seekers resemble those of Deep Ecology. But followers of the Goddess express far more anger toward our male-dominated culture. To save the earth, they plan to . . .

☐ Replace the obsolete patriarchal system of a Father God which, they say, is squeezing our planet dry of resources, with the more compassionate culture of the ancient Mother Goddess.
☐ Revive the ancient myths, images, and rituals of the Goddess.
☐ Reclaim the power and sacredness of eroticism.

Ecofeminism develops the connections between ecology and feminism that social ecology needs in order to reach its own avowed goal of creating a free and ecological way of life.[5] (Ynestra King in *Healing the Wounds*)

Ecofeminists envision a world without authority figures — or male saviors, "for the saving and sustaining power is in herself."[6] Filled with earth's psychic energies and wisdom, we would each be free to do our own thing.

But would we? History proves the opposite. More than

4,000 years ago, Goddess worship flourished in Sumeria/ Babylonia, present-day Iraq. It spread throughout the Near East, then branched off to North Africa, Asia, and Europe. Its occult practices followed. Those who look behind the mythical facade today will still find the same cluster of occult tools: divination, magic, "sacred" sex, various kinds of sacrifices, and spiritism—along with their corresponding armies of hostile, tormenting spirits. (See charts in chaps. 8 and 9.)

Contemporary Goddess spirituality draws inspiration from all the variations of earth-based religions, including Native American Spiritism, which isn't matriarchal at all. It also embraces European nature religions (essentially witchcraft), Westernized Hinduism, Chinese Taoism, Japanese Shintoism, and Buddhism whose quest for self-realization and aversion for logic fits right in. Many differences and contradictions are simply ignored. "A Gaian Buddhism," writes Elizabeth Roberts in *Dharma Gaia*, "reminds us that we are the Earth."[7] All these influences are merging and multiplying in today's self-seeking, power-hungry, post-Christian Western culture. (See chart 5.)

As the pagan religions of the world converge in our midst, the social transformation is accelerating. Look at a few testimonials to the rising power of the Goddess:

☐ During exam time at Pennsylvania's Bryn Mawr women's college, votive offerings accumulate at the feet of a statue of Athena, the Greek Goddess of wisdom. "Everybody does this to bring good luck,"[8] said Emily Cotlier, a sophomore from Connecticut. Sharing Athena's adulation is a large bust of Juno, the Roman Goddess of fertility and celestial light, who supposedly wields power over the climate. According to the *New York Times*, "Gifts to these Goddesses are signs of a growing interest in pagan traditions."[9]
☐ In a large room sparkling with crystals, candles, flowers, and witchcraft books, the *Christian Association* at the University of Pennsylvania gathered hundreds of women (of varying ages, religions, and sexual orientations) for four hours of women's rituals led by Starhawk. Geela Razael Raphael, a rabbinical student, helped organize the event.[10]

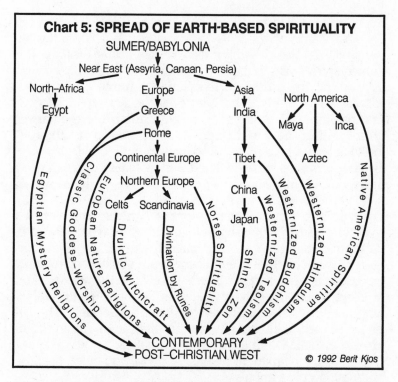

Chart 5: SPREAD OF EARTH-BASED SPIRITUALITY

© 1992 Berit Kjos

☐ In 1991, more than 160 American colleges and universities were offering majors in Women's Studies, a fast-growing field that examines and promotes the goals and writings of the feminist movement including feminist history, politics, and psychology, reproductive rights and abortion, lesbianism and sexual relationships, ecofeminism, witchcraft, goddess-spirituality, and other views discussed in this book. This movement is not all neopagan, but it has drawn many young women away from the Church toward feminine spirituality.[11]

☐ A California middle school labeled an entire library section *Witchcraft*. Another section, titled *Religion*, contained books on Buddhism, Hinduism, Native American Spiritism, etc., but none on genuine Christianity. Two books showed how witches supposedly saved England from Nazi invasion during World War II: a coven of witches "cast a circle" on the coast, raised a "cone of power" with their thoughts, then projected those thoughts against Hitler.[12]

☐ The theme of the 1991 World Council of Churches assembly was *The Holy Spirit and the Renewal of Creation.* But which spirit was guiding keynote speaker Dr. Chung Hyun Kyung of the Korean Presbyterian Church? Surely not God's! To her, the Holy Spirit was the Korean *Goddess* of compassion and wisdom. How did church representatives from around the world respond? After *summoning* the (unholy) spirits of earth, air and water—and of victims (she listed numerous women including witches) oppressed by Judeo-Christian teachings and other forms of tyranny, Dr. Chung received a standing ovation.[13]

☐ A statue of the Greek Goddess Athena "represents a symbolic rebirth of Nashville,"[14] declared Mayor Bill Boner, as thousands of viewers celebrated the unveiling of the forty-two-foot statue, a magnificent replica of the statue that once dominated Athen's Parthenon. Like the waxing and waning moon, the eleven snakes on her breastplate symbolize life and renewal to those who love the Goddess. The gift shop teemed with people buying eight-inch Athena figurines, demonic-looking masks, T-shirts bearing her likeness, and jewelry shaped like snakes, owls, and goat heads—popular occult symbols.

The Goddesses of Greece with whom we are most apt to be familiar—Hera and Athena, Aphrodite and Artemis . . . —are participants in a polytheistic pantheon dominated by all-father Zeus. . . . They are highly developed and specialized forms of the primordial Mother Goddess. The Greeks called this Goddess of the beginning Gaia which means earth.[15] (Christine R. Downing)

The Reigning Goddess.

"Was a peaceful matriarchal world shattered by patriarchal invaders?"[16] The *New York Times* posed this question in a 1990 article featured in its science section. In the article, "Idyllic Theory of Goddesses Creates Storm," Peter Steinfels reviewed *The Language of the Goddess,* which built a questionable framework for an explosion of popular Goddess speculations. In the book, archeologist Marija Gimbutas presents a history lesson which delights today's growing force of ecofeminists, environmentalists, and mythologists.

Long ago, explains Dr. Gimbutas, when matriarchal societies worshiped Goddesses, people lived in harmony with one another and with nature. Queen-priestesses ruled clans and shunned war. But, somewhere around 4000 B.C., patriarchal invaders deposed the life-giving Goddess and shattered the original peace and equality. In Old Europe, she tells us, waves of Indo-European invaders replaced the nurturing matriarchy with a warlike male-centered dominance.

Forced underground, the Goddess religion maintained a cultural foothold through Greek and Roman female deities, the Virgin Mary, and cultural myths, symbols, and fairy tales. Through the centuries, "a substratum of Old Europe survived in harvest customs and peasant beliefs about springs, rocks, trees, and animals, in medieval magic and the practices that Christian authorities persecuted as witchcraft."[17] These practices, Gimbutas tells us, offer a source of ancient wisdom that our present destructive civilization must tap in order to combat our alienation from nature.

Dr. Gimbutas' assumptions are based on the discovery of hundreds of early European female figures. In the absence of facts, speculation runs rampant. Who ruled—men or women? To pagan feminists who seek to validate their visions of a matriarchal utopia with historical proof, these silent Goddesses speak volumes. Peter Steinfels seems to agree:

> For some time, feminist writers have been seeking nonpatriarchal mythologies and rituals in Jungian psychology, reconstructed notions of witchcraft, or even in pure creations of the imagination. But Dr. Gimbutas gives them something more: the seeming stamp of science and the reassurance of history.[18]

Dr. Gimbutas' fan club is not limited to women. Joseph Campbell wrote the foreword for her book. Anthropologist Ashley Montague hailed her book as "a benchmark in the history of civilization."[19] Environmental theologian Matthew

Fox promotes her philosophy in his quarterly magazine on earth-centered spirituality, *Creation*, and in his lectures to churches and environmental groups across the country. And, speaking for a multitude of men, editor of *Healing the Wounds: The Promise of Ecofeminism* says, "More and more men are embracing ecofeminism because they... realize that in shedding the privileges of patriarchy they do more than create equal rights for all; that this great effort may actually *save the earth* and the life it supports."[20] (emphasis added)

One Goddess, Many Names.

What do the resurging myths of feminine spirituality tell us? Who is this awakening Goddess?

Her names span time and space: Ishtar (Babylon), Astarte (Canaan), Artemis (Greece), Ala (Nigeria), Frigg (Norway). Her personalities range from the loving Venus to the raging, blood-guzzling Kali (India). Yet, behind her many masks, the Goddess represents one basic belief system.

"Every female divinity... may be regarded as only another aspect of the core concept of a female Supreme Being," says Barbara Walker in *The Woman's Encyclopedia of Myths and Secrets*. She blames male writers for breaking the "the Goddess figure down into innumerable 'goddesses,' using different titles or names she received from different peoples at different times.... Yet, such classification tends to disintegrate under deeper study that reveals the same... characteristics in nearly all the 'goddesses.' "[21]

Myths from around the world picture Mother Earth as the universal parent. American Indians recount her emergence from the "womb of the earth."[22] Siberian reindeer hunters carved little figurines of Mother Earth to buy her protection. A Hindu priest sent a dead man on his journey with this advice, "Go, seek the earth, that wise kind mother of all."[23]

To primal cultures, she was the fountain of fertility and the spring of life. Exaggerated breasts, buttocks, and genitals define her as sensuality and sex personified. Some called her the Lady of the Animals and made images that showed part woman, part animal. Others titled her Snake Goddess,

Bird Goddess, the Mistress of the Waters, the Pregnant Vegetation Goddess. Each name addressed a deity (and its corresponding demonic spirit) intimately connected to the daily operation of the earth. No wonder the Mother Goddess became the universal replacement for God our Father.

> [In] the mother-goddess religions . . . the world is the body of the Goddess, divine in itself, and divinity isn't something ruling over and above a fallen nature. There was something of this spirit in the medieval cult of the Virgin.[24] (Joseph Campbell)

Babylon's Mysterious Prostitute.

The written story of the Goddess began in ancient Sumeria, Mesopotamia, and Babylonia—three nations nestled between the Tigris and Euphrates Rivers. The Sumerians called her Inanna; she was both sister and lover of Shamash, the sun god. But by the year 2000 B.C. when Abraham journeyed through this territory on his way from Ur to Haran, the conquering Amorites had swept through the region, established Babylon as their capital, and renamed the Goddess Ishtar.

Ishtar, Queen of Heaven, represented fertility and victory, and was no stranger to war. For more than a millennium, her "sacred" prostitution cult with its profane sexual practices marked and molded cultures in a multitude of nations. Indeed, "she was the universal Goddess par excellence!"[25]

"Ecstatic hymns and songs were sung in her temples throughout the Near East," writes Elinor Gadin. Inanna inspired "the world's first love story . . . tender, erotic, shocking, and compassionate."[26]

Her horrendous religious practices were opposed to everything God had taught His people. In Canaan as elsewhere, Ishtar's temple worship included astrology, spiritism, sorcery, sexual perversion, prostitution, and ritual murder.

The people of Canaan called the Goddess Asherah and Astarte (and sometimes Anath or Ashtoreth). In early years, Canaanite mythology presented two distinct Goddess personalities, but in practice (and in later myths) they merged into one. In essence, she remained Ishtar, Queen of Heaven—the Babylonian Goddess garbed in Canaanite costumes.

Today as then, explains Carl Olsen in *The Book of the Goddess Past and Present,* the Goddess "attracts us with her alluring charms, arouses our curiosity about her powers, and tempts us with her pleasureful and unbridled nature."[27]

Mystery Babylon.

Most Americans today seem oblivious to the claims of the Goddess, yet the world is embracing her values. Keep in mind, this transformation doesn't require conscious assent to or even awareness of the Goddess herself—only a tolerance for what she represents *(Romans 1:21-32)*. Even Christians may simply follow along with media and classroom promotion of her philosophy and slip into conformity. Current statistics on abortion, AIDS, addictions, and violence reflect the consequences of rejecting God and accepting her unholy standards—which have always matched the basic inclinations of human nature *(Galatians 5:19-25)*.

Could these ominous trends culminate in a global embrace of Babylonian spirituality? Is there a relationship between the revival of Babylonian spirituality and the prophesied rise of Mystery Babylon? Are these questions even relevant today?

They are. Though God hasn't told us His precise timing of end time events, He repeatedly reminds us to be watchful and alert to coming signs *(Matthew 24, Mark 13, Luke 21)*. He also urges us to consider the relevancy of the Bible's last revelation—the visions shown to the Apostle John on the Island of Patmos. "Blessed is the one who reads the words of this prophecy, and blessed are those who hear it and take to heart what is written in it" *(Revelation 1:3)*.

Apparently God wants us to be mindful of future events—even though the wait tests our patience. For example, Babylonian spirituality has waxed and waned throughout history, tempting us to believe that today's spreading delusion is simply the peak of another curve. After all, evil times and doomsday prophets have come and gone. Why should this time be different from others?

Second Peter 3:3-4 gives us a clue. Notice that this attitude of skepticism will prevail in end times: "In the last days scoffers will come, scoffing and following their own evil desires. They will say, 'Where is this "coming" He promised? Ever since our fathers died, *everything goes on as it has* since the beginning of creation' " (italics added).

Look again at Babylonian spirituality. You have seen that the universal Goddess is no respecter of gender. Her earthy allurements seduce men as well as women, church members as well as cultists. Just as Christ's *bride* includes the whole Church, so the spirit of the Babylonian *prostitute* gathers an all-inclusive, international army of followers. (See Chart 5.)

As the West joins the East in loving the Goddess philosophy and adopting her practices, it becomes increasingly blind and hostile to God and His truth. America's centuries of freedom from persecution—unusual in the span of world history—could be ending, unless God intervenes. Legal, educational, political, and social injustices toward Christians indicate that the age-old pagan hatred toward Jesus Christ which has smoldered underground for centuries can quickly be fanned into a fiery assault on God's followers. Revelation 17:4-6 reminds us that it will happen—perhaps soon:

> The woman was dressed in purple and scarlet, and was glittering with gold, precious stones and pearls. She held a golden cup in her hand, filled with abominable things and the filth of her adulteries. This title was written on her forehead: MYSTERY BABYLON THE GREAT, THE MOTHER OF PROSTITUTES AND OF THE ABOMINATIONS OF THE EARTH.
>
> I saw that the woman was drunk with the blood of the saints, the blood of those who bore testimony to Jesus.

If this persecution happens in our lifetime, we had better be ready. One part of our preparation is simply knowing what God has told us about future events, so that we won't be surprised. "You know well that the day of the Lord will come like a thief in the night," wrote Paul. "But you . . . are not in darkness so that this day should surprise you like a thief. . . . So then let us not be like others, who are asleep, but let us be alert and self-controlled" *(1 Thessalonians 5:2-6)*.

The Book of Revelation offers some fascinating glimpses into the future. Revelation 13 previews the rise of the world ruler some call the Antichrist, the consequent persecution of Christians, and the coming world government which will require everyone to worship Satan's puppet ruler and to bear his mark, 666. He will win global acclaim because he wears the scar of a fatal wound, proof to the masses that he died and returned to life.

Revelation 17 takes us back to pre-Antichrist days. Here we see the great Babylonian prostitute riding into power on the back of the ten-horned beast "who once was, *now is not*, and yet *will come*" (italics added). The flashy, lustful Babylonian spirit is seducing a world that is ripe for counterfeit enticement. Blinded by her charms, all nations fall victim to a global delusion (also prophesied in *1 Thessalonians 2:9-10*) and enter the first stage of Satan's final onslaught. Yet John sees no harmony between the licentious prostitute and the tyrannical world leader—two warring sides of Satan's dark kingdom.

> The angel said to me; "Why are you astonished? I will explain to you the mystery of the woman and of the beast she rides.... The beast, which you saw, once was, *now is not*, and *will* come up out of the Abyss and go to his destruction. The inhabitants of the earth whose names have not been written in the book of life from the creation of the world will be astonished when they see the beast....
>
> "The waters you saw, where the prostitute sits, are peoples, multitudes, nations and languages. The beast ... will hate the prostitute. They will bring her to ruin and leave her naked; they will eat her flesh and burn her with fire. For God has put it into their hearts to accomplish his purpose by agreeing to give the beast their power to rule, until God's words are fulfilled. The woman you saw is the great city that rules over the kings of the earth" *(Revelation 17:7-8, 15-18)*.

Do you see God's sovereignty in the midst of evil? The

Babylonian spirit will draw people and nations around the world into her licentious and violent lifestyle. Then, with the rise of the Antichrist, there will be a bloody (but welcome) transfer from wild immorality to oppressive order. Yet, the evil intentions of Satan's last puppet will accomplish God's purpose: to crush the corrupting practices of the Babylonian prostitute *(Daniel 11:37-38,* KJV).

Revelation 13 gives the details. There we see the Antichrist rising out of the Abyss to exalt himself as the sole object of worship. His demonically empowered image will desecrate the temple, and all who refuse to bow to him will be persecuted—until Christ returns to receive those who trusted Him.

WHAT CAN FAMILIES DO?

☐ Discuss . . .
1. The myth of prehistoric harmony under the Goddess.
2. Relevant prophecies concerning Babylon.
3. Babylon's seductive spirituality.
4. The consequences of loving the Goddess.
5. Helping others turn to God.
☐ Choose a family project from the list on pages 170–175.

1. THE MYTH OF PREHISTORIC HARMONY UNDER THE GODDESS. Did a prehistoric earth once enjoy perfect harmony under feminine leadership? This feminist myth, often presented as fact, has no factual basis. Only under God's kind reign before the Fall, did the earth ever enjoy perfect peace—but it lasted only a moment in time. When Adam and Eve followed their human nature rather than their Creator, everything changed. While a remnant of pre-flood believers walked with God, most people turned away. God's heart ached as He saw "how great man's wickedness on the earth had become, and that every inclination of the thoughts of his heart was only evil" *(Genesis 6:5).* To rescue His creation from total corruption, He sent the Flood.

Human nature has not changed. Since the beginning of time, man has sought fulfillment in earth-based spirituality.

Without God's truth as our foundation, we are just as vulnerable today to spiritual deception and its consequent corruption.

2. PROPHECIES CONCERNING BABYLONIAN SPIRITUALITY. The following Scriptures offer insights concerning paganism and its consequences. Read and discuss these verses. (One or two per day may be enough.) What basic elements of paganism do you see in each? Genesis 3:1-13; Exodus 32:1-8; 1 Kings 11:5-9, 14; 2 Chronicles 33:1-9; Psalm 106; Proverbs 1:29-33; Isaiah 1:1-4, 29-30; Romans 1:21-32; Revelation 17.

3. BABYLON'S SEDUCTIVE SPIRITUALITY. Who is this mysterious Babylonian prostitute? We can uncover some of her secrets by tracing her nature and influence through the millennia. From the beginning, Babylon flaunted her characteristic pride and the idolatry of earth-centered spirituality. The two fit together.

> When an idol is worshiped, man is worshiping himself, his desires, his purposes and his will. . . . As a consequence of this type of idolatry, man was outrageously guilty of giving himself the status of God and of exalting his own will as of supreme worth.[28] (Otto Baab)

Around 2230 B.C., Noah's great-grandson, Nimrod, ruled the people living in the fertile Babylonian/Sumerian valley. Living up to his name, which meant "Let us rebel," he steered his people away from God. Within a few generations, the people were worshiping gods and goddesses linked to the "host of heaven" (the sun, moon, stars, and planets). The astrological zodiac with its occult divination had supplanted God's loving guidance.

Dr. Henry Morris, founder of the Institute of Creation Research, underscores the monumental influence of Babylon's original idolatry:

> How much of this new system of religion came by direct communication with Satan himself we do not

know, but there is abundant evidence that all forms of paganism have come originally from the ancient Babylonian region. The essential identity of the various gods and goddess of Rome, Greece, India, Egypt, and other nations with the original pantheon of the Babylonians is well established. These pagan deities were also identified with the stars and planets—"the host of heaven." ... This system was formalized in the zodiac.[29]

Through the years, God watched the people of Babel pursue their own arrogant goals. But when they determined to build a tower up into heaven "to make a name for themselves," He intervened *(Genesis 11:4)*. They were using their God-given potential to exalt themselves rather than their Creator, thus isolating themselves further from the only One who could meet their deepest needs. To prove the futility of their grandiose schemes and perhaps draw some back to Himself, He confused their languages. The people scattered and abandoned the symbol of their counterfeit unity.

God's warning fits our times, "If as one people speaking the same language they have begun to do this, then nothing they plan to do will be impossible for them" *(Genesis 11:6)*. Now as then, we are building a unified world based on a humanistic illusion: that mankind can muster the wisdom and power to control natural forces, reach into highest space, and create global unity. Let us not forget what God has shown us: that a united world under a presumptuous leader, who refuses to submit to the Master, would bring terror and tyranny.

The Babel fiasco didn't end human self-seeking. The next few centuries witnessed the rise and spreading influence of the Babylonian Goddess. Apparently, the Goddess was designed to be a feminine imitation of God—an alluring usurper of His authority over man and nature. Surely Satan, playing puppeteer behind the scenes, inspired her insolent boast:

In the brilliant heavens, to give omens in abundance, I appear, I appear in perfection. With exultation in my supremacy, with exultation do I, a Goddess, walk supreme. Ishtar, the Goddess of evening, am I. Ishtar the Goddess of morning, am I. Ishtar, who opens the portals of heaven in my supremacy.[30]

Like Isis of Egypt and Persephone of Greece, Ishtar descended into the underworld each winter to release and unite with her beloved. She always returned pregnant—bringing the promise of a bountiful harvest.

Each New Year, the sexual rites of Ishtar's harlot-priestesses celebrated her mythical reunion with Tammuz or Dumuzi, her consort. (Some myths present Tammuz as her son, a counterfeit infant savior on the lap of his mother). Human sacrifices and other bloody rituals included in the ceremony suggest that the Goddess was a cruel lover "who refreshed the earth's fertility with [her consort's] blood."[31]

Eventually, the incredible moral corruption compelled God to act. First, He used Babylon to discipline His own Israel who had copied Babylon's religious system. Then He dealt with Babylon for its spiritual prostitution and cruelty to His beloved people.

Earth-based religions, led by demonic forces, *always hate those who love God.* Today Babylon's fire of hatred has flared again and awaits the completion of God's irrevocable judgment.

4. THE CONSEQUENCES OF LOVING THE GODDESS. Longing to provide His best for His people, God told Israel to shun the practices of its pagan neighbors. But Israel didn't listen. Like a willful child who refuses to hold his father's hand, it rushed into the pagan traffic—and was crushed.

The "natural" lifestyle of the Goddess was simply too tempting for mankind. Women adored Asherah the Queen of Heaven, men prostituted themselves for her, and families worshiped her at home, on hilltops, and under the trees. Heartbroken, God withdrew His protection and allowed Israel's enemies to occupy the land. The Northern Kingdom fell first in 722 B.C.

> Shalmaneser king of Assyria . . . captured Samaria and deported the Israelites to Assyria. . . . All this took place because the Israelites had sinned against the LORD their God. . . . They set up sacred stones and Asherah poles on every high hill and under every spreading tree. At every high place they burned incense. . . . They imitated the nations around them although the LORD had ordered them, "Do not do as they do." . . .
>
> They bowed down to all the starry hosts, and they worshiped Baal. They sacrificed their sons and daughters in the fire. They practiced divination and sorcery and sold themselves to do evil (2 *Kings 17:3, 6-7, 10-11, 15-17*).

In the Southern Kingdom of Judah, kings like Jehoshaphat and Josiah tried to abolish temple prostitution, ban pagan priests, burn all the Asherah poles, and return to God. But the few periods of peace under God's loving protection never lasted long. The pagan influences had become like a cancer on the land. Again and again God's prophets brought warnings of coming ruin, but the people refused to listen.

> Then all the men who knew that their wives were burning incense to other gods . . . said to Jeremiah, "We will not listen to the message you have spoken to us in the name of the LORD! We will certainly do everything we said we would: We will burn incense to the Queen of Heaven and will pour out drink offerings to her" (*Jeremiah 44:15-17*).

Sometimes the innocent die in the crossfires of rampant evil, and we wonder how a sovereign God who allows suffering can be good. We forget that our limited vision cannot possibly see all of God's plan—anymore than a baby can understand why his parents permit the painful sting of an innoculation.

God's purpose reaches far beyond this life. His justice is carried out in eternity, not in the brief span we call time. Hear God's wisdom through Isaiah's kind but sad words:

"The righteous perish, and no one ponders it in his heart; devout men are taken away, and no one understands that the righteous are taken away to be spared from evil. Those who walk uprightly enter into peace; they find rest as they lie in death" *(Isaiah 57:1-2)*.

5. HELPING OTHERS TURN TO GOD. God is both sovereign and just. He rules nations and controls climates. He has shown us which kinds of lifestyles lead to health and happiness and which lead to destruction. He wants us to know Him as He is—our caring Father who sees the dangers ahead and longs to lead us to safety.

"There is no God apart from Me," He tells us, "a righteous God and a Savior; there is none but Me. Turn to Me and be saved, all you ends of earth" *(Isaiah 45:21-22)*.

Notice the key difference between our God and all others: None of the world's gods or goddesses offer people a personal, caring relationship. Unlike our Shepherd who gave His life for us, the fearful, angry gods and goddesses of nature religions demand sacrifices and self-mortification (cutting oneself to gain divine sympathy was common to Babylonian as well as Baal priests, to Asian as well as Sioux Indians). Fear, not love, impelled worship.

Our God doesn't demand sacrifices from us. He *became* the sacrifice that frees those who trust Him from two kinds of oppression: *bondage* to sin and the *penalty* of sin. He calls everyone to come and receive—not through our work, talents, or human effort—but by faith alone. To those who come, He gives His resurrection life—the assurance of peace in the midst of turmoil, wisdom in our confusion, strength in our weakness. But remember the difference: What God promises to those who trust and follow Him, Satan falsely offers to *everybody*. Be sure you know the Shepherd's voice from the counterfeit. Study John 10:1-18.

Remember, people turn away from God. He doesn't turn from them. Humans may accuse Him of being exclusive, but His *inclusiveness* invites *all* people to come and receive from His abundance. He waits with open arms for anyone—no matter how decadant, broken or wounded—to come. All they need to do is to confess their sins, acknowledge their need, trust in His love, and receive His life. He will embrace and welcome them into His family.

How then do you persuade the deceived to come to Jesus? Tell them about your relationship with Him. Most people who are trapped in deception will resist your biblical arguments, but they may be longing for such a relationship. Remember, a capricious Goddess or an impersonal force does not *love* its subjects. So tell—and show by your example—the exciting message: God loves you! Share what He is doing in your life from day to day. Explain that Jesus Himself is *the way* to peace and victory. "If you confess with your mouth, 'Jesus is Lord,' and believe in your heart that God raised Him from the dead, you will be saved" *(Romans 10:9).*

> Your love, O LORD, reaches to the heavens,
>   Your faithfulness to the skies.
> Your righteousness is like the mighty mountains,
>   Your justice like the great deep...
> How priceless is Your unfailing love!
>
> *(Psalm 36:5-7)*

SIX

The Goddess in Every Person?

The conventional notion of the self ... is being replaced by wider constructs of identity and self-interest—by what you might call the ecological self or the eco-self, co-extensive with other beings and the life for our planet. It is what I will call "the greening of the self."
—Joanna Macy, "The Greening of the Self"[1]

Natural evolution [is] part of a deeper spiritual evolution of consciousness ... divinity within all of us emerging more fully into manifestation, resulting in a broader, deeper sense of Self.
—Mike Wyatt, *Green Synthesis*[2]

Pride is their necklace. . . . Their mouths lay claim to heaven, and their tongues take possession of the earth. Therefore people turn to them and drink up waters in abundance. (Psalm 73:6, 9-10)

A CHARMING LITTLE BOOK called *The Magic Locket* has touched the hearts of millions of little girls with the seductive message of the Goddess. On its peach-colored cover is a heart-shaped locket, and inside the golden heart hides a wonderful surprise. Through this surprise, a clumsy little girl learns the secret of her human potential. And what is it?

"It is a magical locket," says Aunt Emma. "If you wear it, it can help you do whatever you want. That is, if you believe in it."[3]

The little girl believed. "I believe in you," she said as she held the locket tight the next morning—and the next—and each day after that. Her faith transformed her life. Now she could do anything—perfectly.

One day the little locket flew open and revealed the magic formula: A tiny mirror which reflected her own image. The message? "Why it's me!" thought the little girl. "It's really me. *I'm* the magic in the locket."[4]

Recognize that we all come from the same life-force, equipped with the potential for helping ourselves to become fully evolved. . . . Be aware that you have energy to use for yourself. This energy comes from the center of the earth, it moves through your feet and legs and grounds you. . . .

Now say to yourself, "I am able, I can do this. I have the energy through my groundedness, my relationship to the heavens and my interconnectedness with others. I am able."[5] (Virginia Satir, *Meditations and Inspirations*)

In his book *The Finale*, Calvin Miller tells a similar story — but from a Christian perspective. The main character is called Dreamer, the earth is Terra, and Satan is the World Hater alias The Prince of Mirrors. This Dark Prince comes to tempt Dreamer:

"I am the only hope for days ahead. I've come to turn the world from war and bless Elan's pursuit of ore that promises to keep our planet strong and free . . . I guard and shall redeem the universe that slumbers just above the waiting curse."

The magnetism of his words of warlike peace drew Dreamer. He wanted to believe, yet knew he had to ask, "But how do you redeem?"

The giant lowered kind eyes and extended a massive arm in warm entreaty: "I show you now the portrait of my hope."

He drew a silvered mirror from his tunic and held it up to Dreamer's face: "Here, Dreamer, is the face of him who sets the planet free."[6]

"I go now into Terra, to tell all of her people my good news! I'll preach to every creature the doctrine of the glass. Terra shall be saved by this clear, final image of herself."

.... The Prince of Mirrors returned from preaching through the Empire. On every continent, men stood enthralled, staring at their images. "We wear one face, behold a common glass," they sang. ...

"Where is your book of truth?" [asked Elan.]

"Here!" the Hater said, pulling the mirror from his pocket. "Here is the doctrine by which men most bend to our control—*man's fascination with himself*. In this small glass is subjugation so complete it wipes away the universe. As long as men behold themselves, they will look no higher."[7]

The Goddess Within.

One day, as I browsed through the special displays in a bookstore, *The Pregnant Virgin* by Marion Woodman caught my eye. Reading from its back cover, I learned that it told "about becoming conscious ... about the wisdom of the body, initiation rituals, dreams ... about relationships and the search for personal identity. It is a celebration of the feminine, both in men and women. It is about becoming free."[8]

"A thinking heart," it said, "can bring us closer to our inner virgin, 'one-in-herself,' forever open to new life, new possibilities—our own unique truth."

This philosophy fits today's mind-set, I thought. *There is no absolute truth; each person merely selects his own favorite myth.*

A woman noticed what I was holding. "That's a great book," she exclaimed.

I looked up. "How did you hear about it?" I asked.

"My psychologist told me to read it. It showed me that co-dependency and my addictions all stem from not getting in touch with my feminine spirituality." She explained how "our male-dominated society" had blocked her awareness of her true self and her power as a woman.

I thanked her for informing me, replaced the book, and prayed, "Lord, what is happening to this world? How did we wander so far away from Your truth? Everything seems upside down, and people don't know You anymore. How can we communicate Your love to people who want their own way?"

Knowing the Goddess-Self.

"It is time to begin writing a new psychology of the feminine, a psychology that returns women to their ultimate roots—a Goddess psychology."[9] In their article, "The Wounded Goddesses Within," Roger and Jennifer Woolger show how this emerging feminine consciousness can lead to the coveted prize, self-actualization: "To know oneself more fully as a woman is to know which goddesses one is primarily ruled by and to be aware of how different goddesses influence the various stages and turning points of one's life."[10]

The Woolgers give Carl Jung credit for discovering the healing and empowering archetype of the Great Goddess—the answer to the yearnings of women today.

Archetype? It took awhile before I grasped the meaning of this word modern psychology has raised into prominence. *The New Lexicon Webster's Dictionary* (1989) defines it as "the model from which later examples are developed, or to which they conform, a prototype." That helps. Evidently Jung saw the Goddess—her forceful, creative, sexual, and spiritual nature—as a perfect model for men and women today: "How different was the former image of matter—the Great Mother—that could encompass and express the profound emotional meaning of Mother Earth."[11]

Becoming the Goddess-Self.

Webster also classifies archetype (here it gets more complex) as "one of the inherited unconscious patterns which Jung held to constitute the fundamental structure of the mind." It can be observed through "images recurring in dreams, behavior patterns, etc."

Dreams and images were important to Jung. They have always been important to Goddess cults. Many believe that dreams and images flow out from some sort of a cosmic pool of knowledge, influence the psyche, and print ancient mythological themes on our subconscious. They say that the Goddess continues to exert her force, push our buttons, and pattern our behavior, whether we believe her or not, so we had better learn to work with her and enjoy the process. Jung called this pool of cosmic wisdom "the collective unconscious." Goddess worshipers call it the Goddess.

What does this mean? To those who follow Jung and the Goddess, healing comes from learning to know and accept yourself as the Goddess in all her various facets: compassionate, angry, loving, erotic, aloof, etc. To develop this self-consciousness, you need to:

☐ Look to the past: study ancient myths and images.
☐ Look to the present: discover your potential.
☐ Be creative: express your Goddess-self through art.
☐ Always remember: *you* are the conscious and visible manifestation of earth's creative energies.

These beliefs are gathering force and becoming a swelling tide. The camouflaged spirit of Babylon has awakened the West to its pagan past. As Elinor Gadon tells us:

> Feminists are turning to the Goddess as a model for self-transformation and empowerment. Women experience power as rooted in their biological selves, an enabling life force in contrast to the authoritative, hierarchical "power over" now so widely instrusive in our society.[12]

To put Jung's teaching into a Christian perspective, we need to remember that much of it came to him through Philemon, his spirit guide (what the Bible calls a *familiar spirit*). Jung's childhood fascination with the supernatural had borne fruit.[13]

In *Revealing the New Age Jesus,* Doug Groothuis tells about Jung's encounter with another deceiving spirit: "In 1916, after experiencing some bizarre paranormal events, Jung wrote in three days a mystical piece called *The Seven Sermons to the Dead,* which he ascribed to Basilides, a Gnostic teacher of the second century in Alexandria."[14]

It is not surprising that Jung, who tapped information from the vast reservoir of demonic knowledge, coined the concept of a *collective unconscious*. Nor is it surprising to see a bond of understanding between Jung and goddess psychology which views the Goddess as a similar source of universal knowledge. Occult formulas (some are described in chapters 2 and 4) open willing minds to both sources of information. In other words, both the Goddess and Jung's *collective unconscious* provide pleasing facades for the vast storehouse of demonic deceptions.

Remember, there are only two sources of supernatural information: God and Satan. Jung rejected the God of the Bible. What he and other pagans heard were the "doctrines of demons" *(1 Timothy 4:1)* that characterize end times. These are the counterfeit promises and distortions of truth which deceive those who don't know biblical truth (2 *Thessalonians 2:9-10*). "Deceitful spirits" whisper these lies into the dreams, thoughts, and meditations of anyone seeking "higher" or mystical knowledge apart from God.

Empowered by the Goddess.
"Dreams and wishes go together,"[15] wrote Virginia Satir, family therapist and founder of Avanta Network, an international organization dedicated to developing techniques for teaching family and professional communication. Satir, whose books have found amazing acceptance among educators, has developed her own blend of empowering imagery, Eastern pantheism, and Goddess spirituality:

> Dreams and wishes can be manifested. Use the power of a golden wishing wand to make it happen. Picture your golden wishing wand in your hand. Endow that wand with the ability to remove your fear of risk-taking. . . . Feel the texture, look at the form. It's yours, for the rest of your life, to use in whatever way you want.[16]

In *Meditations and Inspirations*, she guides her students into a dreamy state of consciousness where they build their own psychic workshop and redesign their lives. How? Through centering, deep breathing, affirmations, focusing, visualizations—the magical formulas of earth-centered spirituality. "I own me," she writes, speaking for the multitude of school children, educators, church leaders, and modern therapists who love her books and teach her message. "Therefore, I can engineer me."[17]

The Creator counters the lie with truth: "You are not your own; you were bought at a price. Therefore honor God with your body" *(1 Corinthians 6:19-20).* And how do we honor God? By allowing Him to fill and lead us—not by engineering ourselves.

Creation worship turns to self-worship. *Occult enlightenment* is a subjective union with the image of God within us. Thus, it is mystical idolatry in the fullest sense of that term. The process of *self-realization* brings the idolator and his idol together as one. Needless to say, such experiences are a supple medium for demonic manipulation.[18] (Brooks Alexander)

"To worship one's self (in self-realization) . . . is, in Christian terms, simple idolatry operating from the usual motive of unconscious egotism,"[19] explains Paul Vitz in *Psychology As Religion: The Cult of Self-Worship.* Like the "broken cisterns" of Jeremiah 2:13, it eventually leads to emptiness and disillusionment.

Self-Idolatry in Schools.

The self-focused message of personal power and connectedness is spreading like wildfire through the educational system. *Nationwide* classroom programs such as Family Life Education teach students to become their own *Persons*—to set aside parental guidelines and take charge of their own lives. Nobody can tell them what to do—other than those who teach this philosophy.

When schools prompt students to put their faith in an evolutionary process that began by chance, children face an identity crisis. Many lose their sense of worth and have no moral standard to guide them. Today educators are desperately searching for new ways to build self-esteem, instill some sort of values, and empower children to "take charge of their lives."

Lottie Beth Hobbs writes in *The Family Educator:*

> All values clarification and decision-making programs (drug and sex education, death education, etc., under a wide variety of titles such as *Quest, Skills for Adolescents, Here's Looking at You 2000, Project Charlie,* and many others) are based in NONDIRECTIVE EDUCATION. For several decades the principle has permeated not only secular education but has been embraced by some churches and religious schools from preschool to postgraduate.[20]

Nondirective education was developed by Dr. Carl Rogers, Dr. Abraham Maslow and Dr. W.R. Coulson. Maslow saw its dangers before he died and tried to correct the damages.[21] His own experiments had shown him that when children learned "self-actualization" and broke loose from the safety of parental boundaries, two things happened: Freed to be *independent decision-makers* who make their own choices, children become unteachable. And without the knowledge and experience to choose wisely, many show little resistance to the onslaught of tempting voices which lure them into dangerous forms of *de*pendence. A contemporary version of Genesis 3:4-5 might sound like this:

"God didn't say you shouldn't do it. He wants you to be happy . . .

"But my dad said . . ."

"Your dad lives in another world. If you listen to him, you'll never learn to live. Listen, you need to find your Self. To get in touch with all your feelings. To express who *you* are. The choice is yours, not his."

"But it doesn't seem right."

"You're supposed to explore the alternatives. Find what fits you. It's okay to feel good. You own your mind and your body."

What happens when children accept no authority but their own? What kind of employees will they make? How will they affect the economy, churches, the family, and God's ongoing work?

One visible result is a growing sense of frustration and

futility bred by unrealistic dreams and unfulfilled expectations. Another is an addictive but futile pursuit of pleasure, which devastates both individuals and cultures. For when self-fulfillment becomes the goal, moral boundaries give way to uncontrollable self-indulgence, promiscuity, perversion, drugs, and violence.

In spite of Dr. Maslow's change of mind and Dr. Coulson's persistent attempts to expose the dangers and turn the tide, classroom promotion of self-actualization continues to spread. Educators like the message: It fits both humanistic ideals and earth-centered spirituality. Tobacco companies like it: The money they pour into programs like Quest multiplies through children set free to buy their products. Planned Parenthood likes it: Youth who had learned to make their own choices (independent of parental guidance or objections) are readily seduced by Planned Parenthood's promotion of free sex—and the resultant abortions.[22]

The Deception Spreads.

Many family therapists like the message of self-actualization. Some, such as John Bradshaw, disseminate it to homes and churches via televisions, books, and videos. "We come to know our beingness—our true self,"[23] says Bradshaw, who calls himself a "Christian theologian" but endorses Virginia Satir's occult beliefs. His "true self" deals with the "domain of higher or *unity consciousness.*" Notice its similarity to Jung's *collective unconscious* and its distortions of biblical truth:

> There is also evidence that *this consciousness is connected to all created consciousness.* The early work of J.B. Rhine at Duke in *telepathy* pointed clearly in this direction. The more recent work of Putoff and Targ at Stanford Research Institute (SRI) on Remote Viewing E.S.P. has offered powerful new data suggesting that once in higher consciousness, we have a higher power available to us. Their belief is that this power results from being *connected to all other created consciousness.*
>
> There are also ancient traditions supporting a higher

power through expanded consciousness. The Indian Medicine Healers believed there was a greater power available through the use of meditation and the fusion with *power animals*. Jesus told His followers that there were powers available to them that were greater than the powers He manifested. His human powers were clearly powers of psychokinesis, clairvoyance, telepathy and *precognition*.[24] (emphasis added)

Bradshaw's second paragraph joins his teaching to all the other current philosophies that draw power and wisdom from occult sources. His views on unity consciousness join it to the vast array of pagan religions based on belief in the one universal mind or force that fills and connects all things. His teaching is especially dangerous because it speaks to a genuine need in our confused, hurting post-Christian culture. It also presents a counterfeit Jesus.

Like Bradshaw, other contemporary teachers and therapists have incorporated a cosmic Christ into their all-embracing spirituality. They help others attain a state of *being* or *becoming* which befit Buddhism and Sufism—but has nothing to do with our identity in Christ or with becoming conformed to His likeness *(Romans 8:29)*. Many listeners are fooled into accepting their teaching as genuine Christianity.

In *Against the Night,* Charles Colson tells us "Those who claim to be Christians are arriving at faith on their own terms—terms that make no demands on behavior."[25] His statement is based on a study by sociologist Robert Bellah, who found that eighty-one percent of Americans agree that "an individual should arrive at his or her own religious belief independent of any church or synagogue."[26] A comment by a woman named Sheila exemplifies this distortion of Christianity: "I believe in God," she said. "I can't remember the last time I went to church. But my faith has carried me a long way. It's a 'Sheila-ism.' Just my own little voice."[27]

Remember 2 Thessalonians 2:10, "They perish because they refused to love the truth." Without a love for truth and a mental storehouse filled with God's Word, people cannot discern error. Many are drawn to the self-focused empowerment of goddess-philosophy and its psychological-spiritual imitations. Like rudderless boats in the night, they cascade down the rapids trapped in a raging social current headed for destruction.

WHAT CAN FAMILIES DO?

☐ Discuss ...
1. The difference between self-realization and knowing Christ.
2. The difference between self-empowerment and God's strength.
3. Our identity *in Christ.*
4. How to surrender to God and follow Him.
☐ Choose a family project from pages 170–175.

1. THE DIFFERENCE BETWEEN SELF-REALIZATION AND KNOWING CHRIST. God warns us not to focus on self and feed its insatiable appetite. "Do not use your freedom to indulge the sinful nature; rather, serve one another in love. ... For the sinful nature desires what is contrary to the Spirit and the Spirit what is contrary to the sinful nature" *(Galatians 5:13, 17).*

Nearly a century ago, Oswald Chambers described our natural tendency to idolize self in contemporary terms. "The disposition of sin is not immorality and wrongdoing, but the disposition of self-realization—I am my own god. This disposition may work out in decorous morality or in indecorous immorality, but it has the one basis, *my claim to my right to myself.*"[28]

Isn't that the issue we are wrestling with today? Who do we belong to—God or ourselves? The Bible is definite. "Whether we live or die, we belong to the Lord" *(Romans 14:8).* Do we have a better pattern for our lives than the one our Maker provides?

Those who follow the Goddess tell us that self-awareness and self-actualization lead to wholeness, healing, and empowerment. That sounds wonderful, but it's simply not true. This focus on self ignites a burning desire for self-

Our Lord's teaching is always anti-self-realization. His purpose is not the development of man; His purpose is to make a man exactly like Himself, and the characteristic of the Son of God is self-expenditure. If we believe in Jesus, it is not what we gain, but what He pours through us that counts. It is not that God makes us beautifully rounded grapes, but that He squeezes the sweetness out of us. Spiritually, we cannot measure our life by success, but only by what God pours through us, and we cannot measure that at all.

"He that believes in Me, out of him shall flow rivers of living water"—hundreds of other lives will be continually refreshed. It is time . . . to cease craving for satisfaction, and to spill the thing out. Our Lord is asking who of us will do it for Him.[29] (Oswald Chambers, *My Utmost for His Highest*)

fulfillment—an objective a person can never attain and which God refuses to satisfy.

2. THE DIFFERENCE BETWEEN SELF-EMPOWER-MENT AND GOD'S STRENGTH. Can humans really create their own imagined reality? Do children have power to make their dreams and wishes—even good ones such as saving the earth—come true?

It is true that God occasionally spoke to His servants through dreams. But more often dreams brought counter-feit messages and false promises—and were fulfilled through demonic, not divine, empowerment:

> If a prophet, or one who foretells by dreams, appears among you and announces to you a miraculous sign or wonder, and if the sign or wonder of which he has spoken takes place, and he says, "Let us follow other gods—and let us worship them," you must not listen to the words of that prophet or dreamer. The LORD your God is testing you to find out whether you love Him with all your heart and with all your soul. It is the LORD your God you must follow, and Him you must revere. Keep His commands and obey Him; serve Him and hold fast to Him *(Deuteronomy 13:1-4).*

Israel didn't listen. Ignoring God's guidelines, the people followed Babylon's self-indulgent practices rather than the God who loved them. Still hoping to draw them back to Himself, God told them what would happen to those who identified with Babylon's beliefs:

> Go down, sit in the dust, Virgin Daughter of Babylon; sit on the ground without a throne.... Listen, you wanton creature, lounging in your security and saying to yourself, *"I am,* and there is none besides me.... Your wisdom and knowledge mislead you.... Disaster will come upon you, and you will not know how to conjure it away *(Isaiah 47:1, 8-11).*

David, God's beloved shepherd, king, and friend, saw the cultural dangers or presumptuous pride, distorted identities, and counterfeit claims. Do you see these signs of a decaying culture today? Do you hear the subtle claims to ownership such as "I own my body. I own my time. I own my tongue..."? Might his prayer fit our nation?

> Help, LORD, for the godly are no more;
>   the faithful have vanished from among men.
> Everyone lies to his neighbor;
>   their flattering lips speak with deception.
> May the LORD cut off all flattering lips
>   and every boastful tongue that says,
> "We will triumph with our tongues;
>   we own our lips—who is our master?" *(Psalm 12:1-4)*

3. OUR IDENTITY IN CHRIST. Our true Master is our Maker Himself. He alone has the wisdom and power to solve earthly problems and satisfy human needs. This healing process begins when we come to Him and receive Jesus Christ as Savior. Joined to Him, we have divine life inside—the very life of God Himself. He makes us "new creations," children of the Father, His holy people, set apart for God *(2 Corinthians 5:15; Galatians 2:20; 1 Peter 2:9-12).* As we immerse ourselves in His wisdom instead of our own feelings, He opens our spiritual eyes to see the unspeakable wonder

of who He is—and how much He loves us.

Seeing ourselves through His eyes, we realize our own worth and can begin to break destructive thought patterns (2 *Corinthians* 10:3-5). To transform our way of thinking, most of us need the persistent prayers and encouragement of Christian friends as well as the strength and guidance of the Holy Spirit. Some may also need Bible-centered counseling.

When I was a new Christian, I battled feelings of failure and worthlessness daily. A wise teacher suggested meditating on God's love promises "day and night" (*Psalm 1*) for one month. She gave me a list:

☐ "I have loved you with an everlasting love" (*Jeremiah 31:3*).

☐ "Fear not, for I have redeemed you; I have called you by name; you are Mine" (*Isaiah 43:1*).

☐ "You are precious and honored in My sight and ... I love you" (*Isaiah 43:4*).

☐ "We are more than conquerors through Him who loved us" (*Romans 8:37*).

☐ "I am convinced that ... [nothing] in all creation will be able to separate [me] from the love of God that is in Christ Jesus our Lord" (*Romans 8:38-39*).

I affirmed those truths each morning when I awoke, as often as I remembered them during the day, and before going to sleep at night. Within a week, I had memorized them, and they began to flow through my mind with little effort on my part. God's Word was becoming part of me. By the end of the month, I was a changed person. Never again have I doubted God's love for me or my worth in His sight. No manmade affirmation can compare with the effectiveness of God's personal promises.

4. HOW TO SURRENDER TO GOD AND FOLLOW HIM. "I am the vine; you are the branches," said Jesus. "If a man remains *in Me* and I in him, he will bear much fruit; apart from Me you can do nothing" (*John 15:5*, italics added).

People today cringe at the word *submission*. After all, our *natural* tendency is to resist taking God at His word. We don't want to submit to anything. But there is no other way to inner peace and outer harmony. Only when He sees our willingness to follow His will, rather than our own, can He freely speak to our hearts. Then He begins to show us the wonders of a healing, fulfilling love-relationship with Himself. There, in the center of His will, we receive the needed strength and wisdom to accomplish His work—including the care of the earth. An old hymn I love expresses this victorious surrender well:

> My Jesus, as Thou wilt:
> O may Thy will be mine!
> Into Thy hand of love,
> I would my all resign.
> Through sorrow or through joy,
> Conduct me as Thine own,
> And help me still to say,
> "My Lord, Thy will be done."[30]

Many of us come to Jesus scarred and broken from painful past experiences. From the world's perspective, our wounds make no sense, for those who don't know God can't understand His deep and wonderful workings in our lives. But from God's perspective, wounds and weaknesses are not all bad. They may be the very agents that He uses to draw His hurting ones to Himself, so that He can transform our lives, prove His sufficiency, and make us one with Himself.

"Come to Me, all you who are weary and burdened, and I will give you rest," whispers our Shepherd *(Matthew 11:28)*. He understands our pain and longs to heal our souls as well as our bodies. But the path takes us through a process of *self-dying* rather than *self-actualization*. Jesus explains: "If anyone would come after Me, he must deny himself and take up his cross and follow Me. For whoever wants to save his life will lose it, but whoever loses his life for Me will find it" *(Matthew 16:24-25)*.

If you or another member of your family are one of His

wounded soldiers, ask that the Holy Spirit will lead you together on the path to healing which Jesus has outlined in Matthew 5:3-10. Take time to study and follow His steps together. Be sure to respond to each of His promises. Share your heart with Him.

Keep turning your mind to God, for He will accomplish the transformation, and prepare you to succeed in whatever He asks of you. Know who He is, what He offers you, and who you are in Him *(Ephesians 1:1–2:10)*. "For in Him we live and move and have our being" *(Acts 17:28)*.

No matter how inadequate we might feel, we know we can count on our Lord to lead and enable. He reminds us, "My grace is sufficient for you, for my power is made perfect in weakness" *(2 Corinthians 12:9)*.

SEVEN

Sacred Sex and Empowering Connections

In our own time ... the Goddess once again is becoming a symbol of empowerment for women ... an inspiration for artists, and a model for resacrilizing woman's body and the mystery of human sexuality. —Elinor W. Gadon[1]

By pursuing your allurements, you help bind the universe together. The unity of the world rests on the pursuit of passion ...
—Brian Swimme, physicist, in *The Universe Is a Green Dragon*[2]

She seduced him with her smooth talk. All at once he followed her like an ox going to the slaughter.... Little knowing it will cost him his life.... Many are the victims she has brought down. (Proverbs 7:21-26)

EXPLORING INDIA in the 1960s, my husband, Andy, and I went to Khajuraho, home to a group of medieval temples. There, ancient artist/priests had carved tier upon tier of couples or threesomes posed in a myriad of sexual unions. Amazed by the apparent message, we wondered if these sensual figures were traces of a worship that viewed eroticism as a path to enlightenment. No guide was there to explain the spiritual significance of Khajuraho's curious blend of temple worship and sexual intercourse. Only in light of today's obsession with sex does it begin to make sense. I hope that the insights we have gained since then will help you understand the forces behind these facts:

☐ An explosion of suggestive and explicit sexual images tantalize Western audiences through television, ads, music, entertainment, and modern mysticism.

☐ Sex and AIDS education curricula encourage children to pursue promiscuity rather than abstinence, immediate gratification rather than permanent commitment, and provide graphic instructions on how to enjoy all kinds of sexual experiences.

☐ "More than half of American women ages fifteen to nineteen have had premarital sex."[3]

☐ A thriving pornography industry provides indescribable photos of women being abused, multiple-partner sex, a battery of hetero- and homosexual poses—and, in more hardcore magazines, scenes of gang rape, torture, bestiality, and rape of children.

☐ Some of America's noisiest social reformers insist on their "right" to federal subsidies for radical and obscene art.

☐ Most Ivy League schools celebrate Gay Awareness Week —"an extended brainwashing session"[4]—but refuse to tolerate contrary opinions.

The Madonna Phenomena.

The world's most popular female singer (over 80 million records sold) is a master at blending sexual and religious imagery. Sporting sensual/spiritual labels (*Like a Prayer,* "Like a Virgin," *The Immaculate Collection*) her musical sensations mingle Christian crosses and feigned innocence with seduction and sexual exploits befitting a pagan goddess. Bisexuality, sadomasochism, autoerotic orgasm, and multiple sex partners . . . anything goes. "Unlike the other, I'd do anything," she sings in "Burnin' Up," "I'm not the same, I have no shame."[5]

She's right about the shame. Appearing on "Nightline" after MTV refused to show her kinky sex video, *Justify My Love,* Madonna told her interviewer that the focus of her video was "the celebration of sex. There's nothing wrong with that!"[6] As for feminists who criticize her boy-toy image, she explained, "But *I* chained myself! *I'm in charge.*"[7] Apparently her admirers agree. Picturing Madonna on their December 1990 cover, *Glamour* counted her among its Ten

Women of the Year "for personifying women's power of self-determination."[8]

How did Madonna grab and hold the attention of American youth and the media? Why do her fans—including millions of young girls—sing her songs and parade Madonna-style underwear as outerwear?

"She's telling me that whatever it is I feel about sex, it's okay. Whatever it is I like, I don't have to be ashamed,"[9] explains Mia Tiemann of Petaluma, California. Record impresario David Geffen adds his insight: She is "the superstar sex goddess of the video generation."[10]

Madonna told Johnny Carson, "I wouldn't have turned out the way I was if I didn't have all those old-fashioned values to rebel against."[11]

Her rebellion against "old-fashioned values" serves Satan's purpose well. To demolish the safe boundaries set by God, he has to persuade the masses that promiscuous sex, like Eve's forbidden fruit, is good, not bad. "You will surely not die," lied the serpent. "[Instead] your eyes will be opened, and you will be like God" (Genesis 3:4-5).

"Madonna Is All; she is a universe of one ... we must adore her because she demands it,"[12] says music editor Harry Sumrall. Though Madonna may not embrace the spirituality of ancient paganism, this shrewd, sexy star shines like a modern Aphrodite—the Greek sex goddess currently acclaimed by ecofeminist, religious scholars, and a myriad of seekers yearning of personal and social transformation.

Transformation through Sex.

A 1990 conference on ecology and religion featured Father Matthew Fox, founder of the Institute on Culture and Creation Spirituality (where Starhawk is a faculty member). I attended the conference, and listened as one of the pastors introduced the Dominican priest: "We ... have gathered to hear a man who is returning the word eros to the presbytery. More than a left-brain attitude toward this conference will be helpful."

Matthew Fox proceeded to share his alluring blend of environmentalism, eroticism, and cosmic spirituality with an audience that obviously delighted in his strange message.

Earlier, in an article published by the *Earth Island Journal*, Fox had summarized his prescription for healing the hurting earth. Notice how he blends truth and deception:

> Unlike Fall and Redemption theology, which is dominant today, Creation Spirituality is not patriarchal, but is feminist. It believes ecstasy, eros, and passion are not curses but blessings. Creation Spirituality emphasizes beauty, not self-denial. It believes compassion, justice and celebration are the goals of spirituality. It emphasizes creativity over obedience. It believes humans are essentially divine . . .
>
> Meister Eckhart taught that "God is a great underground river," and that the world's great religions are all wells tapping into that power. We must unleash the wisdom of all religions—Western and Eastern, as well as Native American and Goddess traditions—to reveal the Cosmic Christ.[13]

The "wisdom of all religions" has now been unleashed in the West. It has brought us face to face with pagan myths that are reshaping beliefs. Yes, we need to understand people from other cultures. But when leaders—and even those who call themselves Christian—promote pagan "wisdom" as our guiding light, we had better test everything we hear with truth and recognize the signs of the deception.

"What should I read to understand what is happening?" I asked Carol Delaney, assistant professor of anthropology at Stanford University. Since she had just given a lecture on patriarchal attitudes toward women, I expected her to recommend a champion for feminine spirituality—which she did: Carol Christ, Associate Professor of Women's Studies and Religious Studies at San Jose State University.

I read Carol Christ's two books, *Womanspirit Rising* and *Laughter of Aphrodite: Reflections on a Journey to the Goddess*. Both describe feminist Goddess-centered spirituality. The latter includes essays by two leading contemporary witches, Starhawk and Zsuzsanna E. Budapest.

Christ calls herself "a priestess of Aphrodite." In the following description notice Aphrodite's rejection of boundaries.

Fully and joyously sexual, Aphrodite remains Virgin in that her sexuality is unbridled, untamed, and her own. Though married to Hephaestus according to Olympian mythology, she is neither submissive or faithful to him. Though she is a mother, her child *Eros,* Love or Desire, is but a reflection of her sexuality...

Her sacred places, like her sexuality, symbolize transformation. Aphrodite is also connected to the Near Eastern Goddess of Renewal and Regeneration, Ishtar.... Like Ishtar, she was served by priestesses who engaged in sacred sexual rituals...[14]

Aphrodite represents the "cosmic life force, associated especially with the transformative power of sexuality."[15] This power evidently has its cruel side. The Encyclopedia Britannica points out that Greek mythology often associated Aphrodite concerned "not with human love in general, but with its darker side: rape, adultery, and incest."[16]

Most ecofeminist, deep ecologist, holistic/visionary scientists, and wiccan voices don't like to discuss the dark side of the Goddess (unless they want to use it to justify their own dark side). To them, her unbridled sexuality means lofty ideals such as liberation and renewal, energy and empowerment, ecstasy and oneness, both with others and with the divine.

> Aphrodite's rituals of love and pleasure are the acts which connect the inner and outer planes...we must actually dance, sing, feast, make music, and love in Her honor. It is with our bodies that we worship Her, and through our bodies that She blesses us. By these earthy rituals the false divisions between body and spirit, between mind and nature, are healed. We find the Sacred within us and all things, within our beautiful, living Mother Earth.[17] (Judy Harrow in *Gnosis*)

Timeless Images and Sexual Rituals.

The power and delights of sex have never been promoted as effectively as through today's mass media. Teasing glimpses beckon from roadside billboards, Sunday morning newspapers, prime-time family television, and mail-order catalogs. Look through the eyes of a teenager at the new comic books and computer game arcades. Ponder the effect of movie ad lines such as one for *Dangerous Liaisons*: "Nasty, decadent fun. . . . A seductive, scary, savagely witty look at the unchanging way of the world." The reversal of values God warns against in Isaiah 5:20 is becoming a reality: "Woe to those who call evil good and good evil."

Obsession with sex is natural to a world without God. People have always tried to manipulate the energy that supposedly controls life and creativity. Believing that human and agricultural fertility can be insured by simulating the reproductive act, earth-based cultures around the world have established rituals that did just that.

Of course, rituals are not all bad. To help His people remember that He (not pagan idols) was their provider, God appointed various annual feasts and festivals in Israel. During the Feast of Harvests in the late spring, the people brought the "firstfruit" of their produce to the temple to thank God for His provision *(Exodus 23:14-16)*.

You can easily recognize counterfeit rituals. They are based on pagan myths and have a common objective: to invoke spiritual power. In other words, man rather than God wields the force—and makes himself god.

"A ritual can be defined as an *enactment* of a myth," explains Joseph Campbell. "By participating in a ritual, you are actually experiencing a mythological life. And it's out of that participation that one can learn to live spiritually."[18]

That's true. Those who build spiritual lives based on myths and rituals, will connect with spiritual forces—but not God's. So when ancient Babylon and other earth-based religions established ritual temple prostitution to win divine favor, they invoked demonic spirits. The price: oppression, disease, and destruction. But people have a tendency to ignore the lessons of history. Therefore, pagan beliefs and rituals keep resurfacing, promoting the same lies and occult powers.

In an article titled, "Cakes for the Queen of Heaven: 2,500 Years of Religious Ecstasy," Dr. Peter Berger explains these sensual rites from a Christian point of view:

The rhythms of nature, particularly the sequences of the seasons and the movement of the stars were suffused with divine forces. . . . The cult of sacred sexuality put one in touch with the divine forces in the cosmos and within oneself. That cult, logically enough, tended everywhere toward the orgiastic . . .

The human being's fundamental religious quest is to establish contact with divine forces and beings that transcend him. The cult of sacred sexuality provided this contact in a way that was both easy and pleasurable.

. . . . The cult provided *ecstasy*. In the throes of the orgiastic sacrament, the individual stepped outside his normal self and the humdrum restraints of ordinary life. He became one with the cosmos, with the gods, and *ipso facto* with his own true nature. He ate the apple and he became divine: what, in the biblical perspective, was the original seduction was also the most archaic experience of "consciousness-expansion."[19]

Reviving the Solstice.

Around the world and through the ages, earth-based religions observed winter solstices with rituals that celebrated conception and rebirth. In the more developed myths of Babylon, India, Egypt, and Greece, the Goddess annually gave birth to the sun or the god it represented. The celebrations included mother/son images that resemble those of the Madonna with Jesus. Again the master-deceiver had planted myths that counterfeited God's plan. That the timing of Christmas coincides with the pagan winter solstice adds to the confusion.

Today the winter solstice and spring equinox are honored through multicultural teaching, classroom celebrations, and community events. With their "inclusive" earth-centered emphasis, they are welcome subsitutes for Christian holidays like Christmas and Easter.

Many reform-minded educators view rituals as a way to empower children, build self-esteem, and raise a new consciousness. Dr. Andy LePage's influential book, *Transforming Education* offers this bit of advice:

Creating rituals for bonding, social transformation, and calling forth energy, would aid in making connections with others and with the earth. Through *hatha-yoga,* students could learn to befriend their bodies and cherish their breath . . . [20]

The Mystery of Tantra.

Hatha-yoga? Pupul Jayakar's book, *Earth Mother,* shed some light on this occult ritual. *Hatha* (force) *yoga* (union) is a combination of physical/sensual exercise and spiritual ritual which is supposed to integrate mind and body and join the person to god. It was grafted into a branch of Hinduism and Buddhism called Tantra—which began as a mystical fertility cult that worshiped the regenerative powers of the Goddess. It flourished between the seventh and thirteenth centuries A.D., leaving relics such as the erotic poses on the temple walls at Khajuraho.

Tantra's more complex secrets were transmitted by the *yogi* (or jogi), who supposedly transcends both natural and moral order. Though he renounces the earth, he indulges in its pleasures with abandon. Note the parallel between his lawless lifestyle and America's shift away from God's wise boundaries:

> To the *jogi* nothing is forbidden. By donning this robe he symbolically renounces the earth and its fruit and frees himself from society and its moralities. The jogi . . . is the magician/sorcerer, the master of alchemy, and the practitioner of the forbidding tantric ritual. He is the astrologer, the palmist, and the juggler, he is the poet, the faithless lover, the seducer of mind and heart. He is also the symbol of awakened man . . . a wild and fearful image explosive with power . . . [21]

Tantra spread through India into Tibet and China. Tibetan Buddhists amplified and preserved the Tantric rituals in their mountain monasteries. When China forced the Dalai Lama and thousands of his disciples to flee their beautiful land, they first brought the Buddhist Tantra back across India and then into the West. Suddenly Buddhist study centers—teaching a form of Tantra fitted to Western tastes—sprang up across the United States.

While the word *Tantra* sounds unfamiliar to most Westerners, everyone has seen some of the symbols: the all-seeing third eye, the yogi seated in lotus position, and the serpent—an essential to most earth-based religions.

The late Joseph Campbell has described the spiritual/sexual steps in Tantric meditation countless times on PBS. It fits right into the body of myths that, according to Campbell, could restore meaning to a meaningless world. Now his devotees can read it in his best-selling books.

> Part of his magic is that the general masses desperately want to believe in what he is saying. And apparently the powers of the media want his message believed as well. . . . The result is that the impact of Joseph Campbell on present day America has been enormous. His influence may outdistance all the gurus from the East added up together.[22] (Tal Brooke, *SCP Journal*)

Remaking God.

Like ancient Israel, today's masses covet a God who will do their bidding and approves of all their actions. Like Matthew Fox, many imagine God simply to be like the Goddess: "tender, embracing, erotic. . . . " They choose to ignore or distort His holiness and righteousness.

The Color Purple, assigned reading for Women's Studies at the University of California at Santa Barbara, remade God to fit pagan feminist demands. Ponder this dialogue. If you saw the movie, you may remember that Shug was the beautiful lover brought home by Celie's self-centered husband. Here Shug is teaching Celie her pantheistic beliefs about God and love. Imagine the appeal to women who don't know the true God:

"I believe that God is everything," say Shug. "Everything that is or ever was or ever will be. And when you can feel that, and be happy to feel that, you've found It . . . "

She say, "My first step from the old white man was trees. Then air. Then birds... But one day when I was sitting quiet... it come to me: that feeling of being part of everything, not separate at all. I knew that if I cut a tree, my arm would bleed. And I laughed and I cried and I run all around the house. I knew just what it was. In fact, when it happen, you can't miss it. It sort of like you know what, she say, grinning and rubbing high up on my thigh."

"*Shug!*" I say.

"Oh," she say. "God love all them feelings. That's some of the best stuff God did. And when you know God loves 'em you enjoys 'em a lot more. You can just relax, go with everything that's going, and praise God by liking what you like."

"God don't think it dirty?" I ast.

"Naw," she say. "God made it. Listen, God love everything you love—and a mess of stuff you don't..."[23]

Running Wild.

Does God indeed delight in people who happily "relax" and "go with everything that's going"? No! God shows us that undisciplined human nature tends to become selfish, frustrated, and unlovable, not self-giving, confident, and delightful. It breeds three companion problems: lawlessness, low self-esteem, and failure.

People who violate God's values may try to avoid guilt by hiding from God or hating Him for His "intolerable" standard. They may try to repress their guilt, compare themselves with worse offenders, or blame others—all of which tend to increase intolerance rather than acceptance of others.

The dark side of the Goddess exposes Satan's depravity. Read the accounts of attempted gang rape in Genesis 19:4-5 and Judges 19:22. Both tell of raging mobs of men demanding certain male guests to ravage. In the latter account, the crazed bisexual throng was given a woman to abuse to death. This horrible story seemed unreal two decades ago. Now, in our post-Christian nation, such sexual violence is becoming a reality. Forgetting that every animal knows how to reproduce, some youth view intercourse as a way to prove maturity. Gang rape has become a substitute for tribal puberty rites.

Our entertainment industry makes it all appear good fun. "It's no accident," writes David Hinckley in the *New York Daily News*, "that when the gratuitous nudity of early-80s films got boring, filmmakers switched to gratuitous violence. Same principle. Just keep it fresh."[24]

We shouldn't be surprised at the spreading decadence of a world that rejects its Creator. God told us long ago that "the sinful nature desires what is contrary to the Spirit, and the Spirit what is contrary to the sinful nature" *(Galatians 5:17)*. The social consequences of trusting human nature are devasting:

> There will be terrible times in the last days. People will be lovers of themselves, lovers of money, boastful, proud, abusive, disobedient to their parents, ungrateful, unholy, without love, unforgiving, slanderous, without self-control, brutal, not lovers of the good, treacherous, rash, conceited, lovers of pleasure rather than lovers of God. . . .
>
> In fact, everyone who wants to live a godly life in Christ Jesus will be persecuted, while evil men and imposters will go from bad to worse, deceiving and being deceived. But as for you, continue in what you learned *(2 Timothy 3:1-4, 12-14)*.

WHAT CAN FAMILIES DO?

☐ Pray, and keep wearing the armor of God.
☐ Discuss:
  1. God's plan for sex.
  2. The problem with promiscuity.
  3. The consequences of rejecting His plan.
☐ Choose a family project from pages 170–175.

1. GOD'S PLAN FOR SEX. God designed sexuality with four goals in mind: (1) to bond husband and wife, (2) for

our enjoyment, (3) to produce children and build a family, and (4) to give us a tiny glimpse of the exceeding joy of being joined to Jesus forever (*Genesis 2:24, 24:67, 33:5, Ephesians 5:22-23; Revelation 19:7-9*).

Our Maker wanted sex to be desirable and fulfilling—a physical expression of a growing emotional and spiritual intimacy. But in this world of blatant immorality, God's plan seems almost too idealistic—even to some Christians. Social pressures, false values, self-centered demands, and conflicting beliefs produce and often sanction unsteady, crumbling relationships—in stark contrast to the stability He offers us. More than ever, we need to encourage each other to honor God in our marriages, to pray for our families, and to teach His ways to our children. They need to know that when God says "Don't!", it's for their good (*Deuteronomy 6:1-9; 11:13-15; Romans 6:11-23*). Their future, the survival of the family, and our nation's health depend on it.

"Sacred sex" as a means to oneness and empowerment is obviously not part of God's plan. Peter Berger explains why.

> The basic presupposition of sacred sexuality was the unity of the cosmos with the divine. It was precisely this unity that Yahwism violently rejected. Yahweh was the God who had *created* the heavens and the earth. As Creator, He stood over and against the cosmos. He was not one with it; therefore, there was no way by which contact with Him could be established by fusing the self with the inner processes of the cosmos.[25]

2. THE PROBLEM WITH PROMISCUITY. To experience love, ecstasy, and spiritual transcendence, people risk bodily harm, emotional tearing, and spiritual emptiness. But promiscuity never satisfies. Like drugs and other addictions, it deepens the loneliness and intensifies the craving for more stimulation.

Because promiscuity and its partners, perversion and pornography, destroy people, weaken nations, and separate us from Him, God abhors them. Again and again, He urges us to follow His guidelines and be safe:

Do not lie with a man as one lies with a woman; that is detestable. Do not have sexual relations with an animal. . . . Do not defile yourselves in any of these ways, because this is how the nations that I am going to drive out before you became defiled. Even the land was defiled; so I punished it for its sin, and the land vomited up its inhabitants *(Leviticus 18:22-25)*.

God is referring to the evil that corrupted Canaan before He turned it over to Israel. How bad was it? " . . . barbarous and thoroughly licentious," writes W.F. Albright in his book, *From the Stone Age to Christianity.*[26]

In the fourteenth century B.C., God led the Israelites into the Promised Land after forty years of wandering in the desert. Weakened by their decadent lifestyle, the Canaanites were ripe for defeat *(Deuteronomy 7:1-6)*. Archeologists have unearthed Hittite manuscripts which allow us to peek behind Israel's enemy lines. Wars and epidemics had sapped their strength. Listen to the prayer of a Hittite king from the fourteenth century B.C.:

What is this, O gods, that ye have done? A plague ye have let into the land. The Hatti land, all of it, is dying. . . . O gods, take ye pity again on the Hatti land! On the one hand it is afflicted with a plague, on the other hand it is afflicted with hostility . . . Hatti land is a weary land. . . . In olden days the Hatti land with the help of the Sun-goddess Arinna used to take on the surrounding countries like a lion.[27]

The gods and goddess of Canaan and Babylon demanded child sacrifice. Perhaps this practice also solved the problem of unwanted babies—those conceived through prostitution and other promiscuous relationships. Could this ancient horror be compared to our rising toll of unborn babies, conceived through promiscuity and aborted as a sacrifice to the "prince of this world"—the demonic force behind the Goddess?

The New Testament declares its condemnation—not of the sinner—but of promiscuous and perverted sex:

God gave them over in the sinful desires of their hearts to sexual impurity for the degrading of their bodies with one another.... Even their women exchanged natural relations for unnatural ones. In the same way the men also abandoned natural relations with women and were inflamed with lust for one another. Men committed indecent acts with other men and received in themselves the due penalty for their perversion *(Romans 1:24-27)*.

3. CONSEQUENCES FOR REJECTING GOD'S GUIDE-LINES: The first consequence is spiritual: separation from God. This is Satan's primary tactic against Christians. When people choose their own way, they forfeit fellowship with Jesus. "Your iniquities have separated you from your God" *(Isaiah 59:2)*. The sad prophecy in Matthew 24:12 warns us that in end times, few will turn back from the dangerous path they have chosen: "Because of the increase of wickedness, the love of most will grow cold."

The second consequence follows: emotional bondage. God "gives us over" to our own meager resources, which are no match for the schemes of Satan and the unruly cravings of our human nature. In spite of man's demand for sexual freedom, once illicit practices are indulged, they trap their victims. No one is immune. "Don't you know that ... you are slaves to the one whom you obey—whether you are slaves to sin, which leads to death, or to obedience, which leads to righteousness? ... You are weak in your natural selves" *(Romans 6:16-19)*.

The third consequence is physical: disease and death. Since illness touches everyone sooner or alter, the faithful as well as the rebellious, people hesitate to connect STDs (sexually transmitted diseases) like AIDS to sexual behavior. But God doesn't mince words. Sexual disobedience together with idolatry lead to disease of the body as well as of the land:

You have defiled the land with your prostitution and wickedness. Therefore the showers have been withheld, and no spring rains have fallen. Yet you have the

> brazen look of a prostitute; you refuse to blush with shame (Jeremiah 3:2-3).

> The LORD Almighty, will send a wasting disease upon His sturdy warriors.... The splendor of His forests and fertile fields it will completely destroy, as when a sick man wastes away. And the remaining trees of His forests will be so few that a child could write them down (Isaiah 10:16-19).

Do these verses apply to us today? Remember 1 Corinthians 10:6-8:

> Now these things [Old Testament consequences for sin] occurred as examples, to keep us from setting our hearts on evil things as they did.... As it is written: "The people sat down to eat and drink and got up to indulge in pagan revelry." We should not commit sexual immorality as some of them did—and in one day 23,000 of them died.

4. GOD'S STEPS TO WHOLENESS. God's patience with us reaches far beyond our understanding. His Father-love compels Him to draw us back to fellowship with Him. The way back is the same for all of us: Confession and repentance (our part), forgiveness and healing (God's part).

First, He begins to touch our hearts with awareness of sin—a most unpopular word these days. Somehow Satan has persuaded most Americans that sin and guilt will somehow disappear if Christians would only stop using those words. The opposite is true. When we violate God's principles, guilt makes us feel unworthy. Having rejected the cross, millions are left in that uncomfortable state. They don't realize that God uses guilt to bring us to repentance—the place where we are ready to receive His healing and forgiving love. When we confess our sin, He fills us with a sense of acceptance and worth. No amount of positive self-talk can accomplish that.

"When I kept silent, my bones wasted away through my groaning all day long," wrote King David. "Then I acknowledged my sin to You and did not cover up my iniquity. I said, 'I will confess my transgressions to the Lord,' and You forgave the guilt of my sin." Forgiven, cleansed and renewed, David ended his song on a note of triumph, "Rejoice in the Lord and be glad, you righteous. Sing, all you who are upright in heart!" *(Psalm 32:3, 5, 11)*

We all face a choice: Whom will we serve—self or God? Romans 12:1-2 show us the winning way: Offer your body to God, and renew your mind with truth. Feed your mind with truth until His warnings and promises become more than second nature.

Study Proverbs together as a family; we reviewed it every few years with our sons. Also, know and discuss the following Scriptures: Psalm 1; 119:9-18, 93, 105.

Don't feed on the seductive images and tempting lies of today's popular movies, music, novels, and ads. "I have made a covenant with my eyes not to look lustfully at a girl," said Job. Discuss Job 31:1; Psalms 97:10; 101:3; Ephesians 5; 1 Thessalonians 4:3-8.

For detailed suggestions on building God's values in children and youth, read chapter 4 in *Your Child and the New Age.* Other chapters provide specific guidelines for choosing movies, television programs, books, and music. One simple question we can all ask ourselves when watching a movie is: "How would the person (any character in trouble) have been better off if he or she had followed God's principles?"

Above all, trust God, not yourself, to accomplish His purpose for you:

> Hold on to the good. Avoid every kind of evil. May God Himself, the God of peace, sanctify you through and through. May your whole spirit, soul and body be kept blameless at the coming of our Lord Jesus Christ. *The One who calls you is faithful and He will do it* (1 Thessalonians 5:21-24).

EIGHT

Transforming Art and Empowering Symbols

All across the land, the basis for a new earth-centered culture is being cast. Artists and poets are turning back to the
earth as a source of inspiration. . . . People are creating new
kinds of personal and community rituals to express their
bond to the earth, viewed once again as the nurturing
mother of all life.
— Brian Tokar in *The Green Alternative*[1]

Art is not only a reflection of our culture, it also serves to
shape and define who we are.
— A Chevron advertisement in *Time* magazine[2]

*Although they claimed to be wise, they became fools and exchanged
the glory of the immortal god for images made to look like mortal
man and birds and animals and reptiles. (Romans 1:22-23)*

DURING THE POPULAR television series, "The Power of Myth,"
Joseph Campbell told Bill Moyers, "The images of myth are
reflections of the spiritual potentialities of every one of us.
Through contemplating these, we evoke their powers in
our own lives."[3] Later, they discussed the artist's crucial role
in spreading those mythical images:

> *Moyers:* Who interprets the divinity inherent in nature
> for us today? Who are our shamans?

> *Campbell:* It is the function of the artist to do this. The

artist is the one who communicates myth for today . . .

Moyers: So shamans functioned in earlier societies as artists do now. They play a much more important role than simply being—

Campbell: They played the role the priesthood traditionally plays in our society.[4]

Artists as priests and shamans? Campbell's radical ideas struck home as I paused for a moment by a jewelry stand at the Phoenix airport. A large serpentine pendant had caught my eye. Above it hung a set of earrings sporting the popular yin/yang symbol. Interesting! Glancing up and down the rows of silver—and gold-crafted ornaments, I counted more than thirty different occult symbols—wizards, ankhs (the occult Egyptian cross), goat heads, the Egyptian scarab beetle, pentagrams. . . .

A few weeks earlier I had talked with students at a Christian middle school about New Age influences. When I mentioned occult symbols, they knew exactly what I meant. Many were wearing them—on their ears, fingers, and T-shirts. They had watched them in cartoons, comic books, and Nintendo games.

As I left the jewelry stand, I thought sadly that even God's special symbols—the cross, stars, His beautiful rainbow—had been distorted to fit mythical messages. It seemed as if our world was falling in love with occult art—and the spirit behind it.

Social Progress through Pagan Art?

The headline for a full-page article in the San Francisco *Chronicle* fit our times: "Puppets for Social Change—The art of protest on S.F. streets." The top picture showed a gigantic puppet named Rage swaying above the mass of demonstrators, its mouth contorted in a scream, its fist gripping a sign proclaiming "NO!" Marching with rage were a surrealistic crow, a sun Goddess, and various mythical monsters. Together they comprised "a walking gallery of feelings that collective members want to express—need to express."[5]

Primal expressions are in. Pagan masks, charms, figurines, and pictures decorate model homes. Mythical and mystical art permeate theatres, art museums, music, libraries, and cultural centers.

Some are genuine masterpieces, showing God's cross-cultural touch. Others disturb our senses, for they express hatred, fear, and despair—the feelings of a rootless humanity searching for meaning. Many simply show passivity. They seem to communicate what today's pagans deny: *People who choose substitute gods live at the mercy of forces they cannot control.*

Why do we have this influx of pagan art? Some of it has aesthetic value. And, like the above puppets, it expresses human emotions and experience to a nation that increasingly focuses on feelings. It can raise our appreciation for cultural diversity and promote social harmony. And it can be used to imprint mythical messages on the American mind. According to a *New York Times* article, it serves "to instruct, to *evoke the deceased,* to house the soul, to be the focus of a ritual."[6]

It *is* reshaping American beliefs. Most of us don't argue with a painting. "Artists can play a unique role in raising our consciousness about the changes that must be made for the healing of our planet,"[7] says Adriana Diaz, faculty member at Matthew Fox's Institute.

The quarterly magazine, *Green Letter,* defined the artist's role in building a new environmentally conscious world:

> The arts speak the language of the senses (through words, images, sounds, form, color, touch, and movement) and often communicate things that cannot be otherwise expressed . . .
>
> Artists have an important role to play in creating a more sustainable society and empowering their communities. Their images and actions can stimulate changes in consciousness and behavior. Free and diverse artistic expressions are vital for challenging people to rethink their assumptions and for educating people about their past, present issues, and future visions.[8]

Seeking Utopia.

In his book, *Escape from Reason,* Francis Schaeffer traced the historical steps toward our current pursuit of a mythical Eden. Here I can only show incomplete glimpses of some of those steps. Look for the two main points:

☐ When people turn from God to secular humanism or naturalism (glorifying nature and denying supernatural interference), they create a spiritual vacuum, which soon attracts counterfeit spirituality.
☐ When people reject absolute truth, they lose their standard for reality. They will believe anything in their futile search for something.

(For a more complete look at the influences that led the Western world away from truth and reason toward today's irrational embrace of Eastern, pagan and occult spirituality, read Os Guiness' *The Dust of Death* and Doug Groothuis' *Unmasking the New Age.*)

Renaissance artists established humanism as a social force, but it reached its pinnacle during the eighteenth century Enlightenment. Literature celebrated the supremacy of man's reason and placed humanity at the center of the universe. Writers and poets denied their need for redemption and proclaimed *man's right to absolute freedom.* The fact that secular science presented humans as mere parts of a machinelike world didn't matter. Philosophers and artists would celebrate their reason and freedom—even if freedom made no sense.

In *How Then Shall We Live?* Schaeffer illustrates the ultimate consequences of this arrogance and absurdity. America would do well to heed his warning:

> Like the humanists of the Renaissance, the men of the Englightenment pushed aside the Christian base and heritage and looked back to the old pre-Christian times. In Voltaire's home in Ferney the picture he hung (in such a way on the wall at the foot of his bed that it was the first thing he saw each day) was a painting of the goddess Diana with a small new cres-

cent moon on her head and a very large one under her feet. She is reaching down to help men.

How quickly all the humanist ideals came to grief! In September 1792 began the massacre. . . . Before it was all over, the [French] government and its agents killed 40,000 people. . . . This destruction came not from outside the system; it was produced by the system. As in the later Russian Revolution the revolutionaries on their humanist base had only two options—anarchy or repression.[9]

Consider the similarity between the Enlightenment and current Green philosophy. To Rousseau, *natural* meant *good.* Nature, no matter how cruel and untamed, determined morality. Freedom and wildness became ultimate goals.

To show the futility of this quest, Schaeffer points to the French painter, Gauguin (1848–1903). Seeking total freedom, Gauguin "deserted his family and went to Tahiti where he tried to find it in the *noble savage.*"[10] The canvas of his last great painting expressed his disillusionment: "Whence Come We? What Are We? Whither Do We Go?"

The secular humanists had lifted God's promise of freedom out of context. They ignored the condition: "If you *hold to My teaching,* you are really My disciples. *Then* you will know the truth, and the *truth will set you free*" (John 8:32, italics added). Genuine freedom cannot exist apart from truth.

Atheistic existentialists did nothing to help. Their futile freedom wilted in the terror of cosmic meaninglessness. We see it today in the distorted faces and bodies of Picasso's art and in the dark, grotesque paintings of modern realism. Some resemble the gruesome images of cruel Goddesses like Kali. Others exude weakness, insecurity, introspection, doubt, pain. . . . Broken people, desperate to understand and find meaning within, scream from the canvases of tell-it-like-it-is artists. The answer is no less devastating: Whatever is, is right!

Where then was hope? Reason had failed. What was left?

"Drugs," suggested Aldous Huxley in *Brave New World* (1932). Mind-expanding drugs would open the door into mystical experience and narrow the gap between our post-Christian West and the pagan cultures of the past. As Os Guiness points out in *The Dust of Death*:

> ... these short cuts [to enlightenment], once discovered, were given the halo of neodivinity. Thus, peyote was divine to the Aztecs, coca to the Incas, soma to the Vedas, and ambrosia to the Greeks ... their use became intertwined in the blurry realms of religion, magic, and illumination.[11]

Huxley also sought answers in Eastern religions and ecology—two strange partners considering that, at their core, Hinduism and Buddhism teach that the physical world (maya) is merely an illusion that the seeker must transcend. Neither science nor practical concern for the earth can grow in such an irrational climate. G.K. Chesterton was right. When people reject God, they don't believe in nothing—they believe in anything.[12]

Since man had already rejected reason as a test for reality, the seeking masses were wide open to the next deception: *Optimistic Evolutionary Humanism*. Julian Huxley's utopian vision was literally "out of this world." You see its offspring expressed in the soft, dreamy, New Age fantasy art—perhaps a welcome relief from the stark, cruel distortions of realism.

We know that drugs, occult meditation, rock music, and other counterculture experiences failed to bring the promised fulfillment. Neither will today's visionary New Age or mystical environmental art and music. Francis Schaeffer sums up the futile journey from biblical truth to nothingness and illusion with this astute observation:

> The significant thing is that rationalistic, humanistic man began by saying that Christianity was not rational enough. Now he has come around in a wide circle and ended as a mystic—though a mystic of a special kind. He is a mystic with nobody there. The old mystics always said that there was somebody there, but the new mystic says that that does not matter, because

faith is the important thing. It is faith in faith, whether expressed in secular or religious terms. ... Modern man is committed to finding his answer ... away from reason.[13]

Back to Mother Earth.

Julian Huxley didn't believe in God. He did, however, believe that "men function better if they *think* that there is a god."[14] So did a growing crowd of environmentalists and eco-theologians. In 1973, Norwegian ecophilosopher Arne Naess coined the term *Deep Ecology*. In a 1982 interview at the Los Angeles Zen Center, he explained that the phrase suggests a cultural shift from science to wisdom. "We ask which society, which education, which form of religion, is beneficial for all life on the planet as a whole, and then we ask further what we need to do in order to make the necessary changes."[15]

Environmental writer and poet Gary Snyder suggested some answers. His book *Turtle Island,* which won a 1975 Pulitzer Prize in poetry, linked Zen Buddhism, American Indian traditions and a string of other Eastern religions to Deep Ecology.[16]

Others echo their call. The Dalai Lama tells us the ancient arts of Tibetan Buddhism will produce the unity needed to heal the earth. He hopes to make Tibet an international haven where all can learn peace and harmony from his followers.[17]

In *Transforming Education,* Andy LePage writes, "When the artist has been awakened in every student, there will be a renaissance of aesthetics in our country which will enable us to understand more deeply the native peoples of our land, and bring us into harmony with the earth."[18]

America seems to be moving back to where it started, seeking meaning in life and power for living in occult wisdom. This revival reaches far beyond deep ecology and contemporary paganism. We are not looking at a phenomenon limited to the Green Movement or radical Goddess worshipers. While languages and idols may differ, essentially the same deception permeates our Western world and links it to the pagan beliefs of the rest of the world.

The Common Language of Art and Symbols.
Since pagan beliefs express the myths and inclinations of
human nature, pagan art speaks a global language. Matthew Fox illustrates this fact with a personal experience.
After he completed a series of lectures at a Mennonite seminary, a woman in an Indian sari approached him:

> "You are the first Christian theologian I have ever
> met," she commented, "who spoke Hindi."
> "Goodness!" I replied, "I was trying to speak English."
> "No," she said, "I mean that you speak in images
> that are thoroughly Hindu and speak to my heart from
> my own deepest Indian roots; and those slides you
> showed from Hildegard (Hildegard of Bingen's twelfth
> century mandalas)—they too, are deeply Hindu."
> I was not altogether surprised by this exchange. I
> knew of the influence of Hinduism on Celtic spiritual-
> ity [withchcraft], and that Hildegard was part of the
> Celtic movement along the Rhine. But I was moved by
> this Eastern woman's power of making connections at
> the level of mysticism. After all, it was the Japanese
> Zen Buddhist Dr. Suzuki who first convinced Thomas
> Merton to take Meister Eckhart seriously, just as it was
> the Hindu scholar Coomeraswamy who first alerted
> me to Meister Eckhart.[19]

Pagan art has two sides: the enticing mystical illusions and
the ugly, shadowy horrors of life under occult guidance. The
latter is about as compatible with "traditional" American art as
heavy metal music is with Beethoven. Not surprisingly, those
who love the shadowy attractions have little affinity for art
that communicates grace, beauty, and harmony.
 The National Endowment for the Arts seems to prefer the
former. A *New Dimension* article, "Art Censors: A Closer
Look at the NEA," compares the art it favors with the art it
censors. You have probably read about some of the art it
funds. Among the worst examples was Andres Serrano's
incredible desecration of a crucifix and mockery of Christ.
 You may also remember ex-prostitute Annie Sprinkle's
"Post-Modernist Porn" show at New York's fashionable

Kitchen Theatre. A mixed audience of well dressed artists, entertainers, and politicians participated in this scene:

> Annie herself was ecstatic. As she chanted prayers to the "spirits of ancient sacred temple prostitutes," a delegation from PONY (Prostitutes of New York) shouted encouragement. Ecstasy spread across Annie's face as she invited the audience to examine her . . . (What followed cannot be published in a family magazine . . .) Overwhelmed by the response, Annie uttered the now immortal line, *"Usually I get paid a lot of money for this, but tonight it's government funded."* Not since Marie Antoinette's "Let them eat cake," has one phrase captured the decadence of a regime so unerringly.[20]

In contrast, what kind of art does the NEA censor? Apparently, it rejects any expression of the "aesthetic criteria that are the foundation of Western culture." For example, the NEA *refused* to fund artist Frederick Hart who created the Three Soldiers for the Vietnam Veterans War Memorial, Washington's most popular attraction after the Lincoln Memorial. Hart worked three years in an unheated studio to complete the magnificent Creation sculptures now adorning the main facade of Washington's National Cathedral.

"The NEA told me what I was doing wasn't art,"[21] he explained.

Why such upside-down values? One major difference between pagan and Christian art is that earth-centered cultures are usually based on myths and natural inclinations, while Bible-centered cultures are based on truth and moral order. Their respective art expresses their opposing values. Artists who promote paganism cannot tolerate the expressions of those who follow God.

> Today's true radicals are the realist painters and sculptors who refuse to conform to the modern art establishment. Going up against this establishment . . . is letting oneself in for the "most intense vilification you can imagine."[22] (James Cooper quoting author Tom Wolfe)

WHAT CAN FAMILIES DO?

☐ Pray for discernment.
☐ Discuss . . .
  1. God's purpose for art.
  2. The misuse of God-given talent.
  3. The power of images and imagination.
  4. Using your imagination as God intended.
☐ Choose a family project from pages 170–175.

1. GOD'S PURPOSE FOR ART. God created artists. Their earliest recorded assignment was to build and adorn His tabernacle, where He first established His presence with man (*Exodus 25–27*). Its design and function shows us the Master's delight in fine craftsmanship and the biblical purpose for art:

☐ to delight and edify.
☐ to bring glory to the Creator.
☐ to show the wonder of His creation.
☐ to illustrate His truth.
☐ to record significant events.
☐ to communicate beliefs to the next generation.

Speaking from an artist's point of view, H.R. Rookmaker explains his standard for exemplary art:

> If we say that love is . . . the supreme norm for art, it certainly affects the subjects we choose, the way we treat them, the forms we give them, the materials we handle, the techniques we employ. In Philippians 4:8 [whatever is true, noble, pure, lovely], Paul formulated this for all of life as well as for art.[23]

2. THE MISUSE OF GOD-GIVEN TALENT. As always, Satan seeks to distort God's gifts to fit his plan and purpose. Art and God's truth enhance each other, but so do art and pagan myth. Together, the latter pair can fashion an imaginary world filled with false hopes, untamed passions, counterfeit gods, and deceiving spirits.

Earth-based religions used art, including signs and symbols, to express their beliefs, worship their deities, and invoke spiritual powers. Imaginative figurines and primitive paintings tell us about volatile earth mothers to be appeased, animals that served as hosts of gods and spirits, and spiritual forces that could be manipulated to meet human needs.

What a contrast to the ever-present God, who always watches over and cares for His people! Those who reject Him for a capricious Mother Earth face the worst of human nature and demonic powers. For example, in the magical universe ruled by Aztec gods and spirits in pre-Columbian days, earth Goddess Coatlicue was mother of all gods and humans alike. But she was no gentle and nurturing parent. Her stone image depicts a decapitated monster of a woman from whose neck spring two serpent heads symbolizing streams of blood. She wore a necklace of hands and shears, while her own hands are serpent heads and her feet eagle claws.

Primitive people around the world were well aware of earth's turbulent tempers and cruel actions—far more so than are today's owners of snug homes and piped-in water. To people who battled droughts, storms, floods, and locusts, Mother Earth and her brood of nature deities were formidable and angry rulers who demanded worship for their favors.

Like other religions that worshiped the Mother Goddess and the Sun God, the Aztecs offered human sacrifices to their gods. A cylinder-shaped stone, on which the victim was stretched and his heart removed, remains as a memento from an era of pure earth-based worship. The human sacrifice was thought to provide nourishment for the sun and for life itself, through the blood and hearts of the victims. . . . In sacrifice, the heart of the victim was extracted with a flint knife, but prisoners were also burned or eaten in a ritual form of cannibalism, not for food but as a sort of communion between men and the god.[24]

Those who saw the bloody sacrifices to Hindu Goddess Kali in *Indiana Jones and the Temple of Doom* can best imagine the horror of this worship. Yet similar patterns for human sacrifice were practiced by the Incas and even by the American Indians. Dr. Clark Wissler describes a Pawnee sacrifice of a virgin to the Morning Star—a practice which ended in the early 1800s after a wise Pawnee leader rescued a young maiden from this terrible death:

> When the ritual required, a war party was organized, purified and sanctioned by serious ceremonies. If the [astrological] signs were pronounced auspicious, this party set out for the enemy's country. The object was to surprise a camp, kill and scalp, but to spare an adolescent girl. The captive was carried home, where she was treated with great respect, attended by women, all in charge of a priest of the ritual. . . . A kind of scaffold was erected, upon which the girl was induced to climb, her hands and feet were bound, then a priest rushed upon her, cut out her heart and offered it to the gods. Afterward her body was laid upon the prairie as a further offering.[25]

As you study the chart on page 138, you will see what social studies and world cultures curricula won't admit: that cruelty, fear, and death have always permeated pagan cultures and their art. Only cultures founded on biblical truth and protected by God Himself have enjoyed freedom from the tyranny of Satan's reign.

3. THE POWER OF IMAGES AND IMAGINATION. Images influence cultures in three ways:

☐ By the value we give them. Carved and painted idols are central to earth-based cultures. Ancient Israel encountered idol worship, including astrology, on every side; therefore, God gave explicit warnings: "Do not become corrupt and make for yourselves an idol, an image of any shape. . . . When you look up to the sky and see the sun, the moon and the stars—all the heavenly array—do not be enticed into bowing down to them" *(Deuteronomy 4:16-19).*

We may not be tempted to *bow* to idols. Our kind of idolatry is more subtle. We practice it by replacing our devotion to the Creator and His *unchanging reality* for created and *changeable images*—either God-made nature or man-made things. Brooks Alexander explains the latter:

> We speak of being driven (or seduced) by the "Image" of success, of beauty, vitality, and the good life, etc. Thanks to the technology of television, those abstract "images" have now become literal and visible; what's more, they come alive and speak to us. . . . Certainly all

Chart 6: COMMON PRACTICES OF EARTH-BASED RELIGIONS[26] © 1992 Berit Kjos								
Religion	Astrol-ogy	Solstice Rites	Spirit-ism	Divi-nation	Magic Sorcery	Human Sacrifice	Sacred Sex	Serpent Worship
Primitive	●	some	●	●	●	some	some	some
Babylon	●	●	●	●	●	●	●	●
Witch-craft	●	●	●	●	●	●	some	●
Egypt	●	●	●	●	●	●	●	●
Hindu-ism	●	●	●	●	●	●	●	●
Budd-hism	●	●	●	●	●	●	some	●
Greece	●	●	●	●	●	●	●	●
Rome	●	●	●	●	●	●	●	●
Celts	●	●	●	●	●	●	●	●
Shinto		?	●	●	●	?		?
Inca	●	●	●	●	●	●	●	●
Aztec	●	●	●	●	●	●	●	●
Am. Indian	●	?	●	●	●	●	●	●
Folk Islam	●	?	●	●	●	no	no	?

of television advertising, and much of television in general, purposely stimulates our craving to possess, thus fitting Paul's most basic definition of idolatry.[27]

☐ By their association. Magic signs, symbols, and drawings are tools used to cast spells and invoke occult powers. While idols in themselves are worthless, they are, says Brooks Alexander, "a mask for demonic entities, and a channel for demonic influence"[28] *(1 Corinthians 10:19-20).* Dabbling in magic or bringing pagan art and symbols into your home can cause spiritual bondage and oppression, especially if they are used in occult rituals. Have nothing to do with them.

☐ By their content. The most obvious effect of art—paintings, sculpture, music, dance—is to stir the imagination, influence thought, and touch the hearts. While God wants to use our imagination to make His truth alive to us, Satan will use our imagination to give an appearance of reality to his mystical illusions.

Frequent exposure to images that violate our moral boundaries will desensitize the conscience and begin to mold the mind to fit the message. Films, plays, stories, and music filled with profanity, sensuality, and violence are not "merely exposing reality." They transform our view of reality. We become like the "art" that fills our mind and vision.

☐ Know and discuss the following verses. Apply them whenever you choose movies, music, pictures or jewelry: Psalm 97:10; Isaiah 5:20; Proverbs 3:7; Colossians 3:1-5; 1 Thessalonians 5:21-23; 1 Timothy 2:9-10. Review Ephesians 5.

4. USING YOUR IMAGINATION AS GOD INTENDED. David, God's beloved shepherd king, wrote the imagery of Psalm 23 based on his intimate relationship with his Lord. When we, like David, allow the Holy Spirit to fill our imagination with images from God's Word, He draws us close to Himself. Focusing our minds on Jesus, we are transformed into His likeness by "beholding" Him *(2 Corinthians 3:18).*

God tells us that we "have no excuse" for not seeing Him: "For since the creation of the world God's invisible qualities—His eternal power and divine nature—have been clearly seen, being understood from what has been made" *(Romans 1:20)*. When we truly know God (primarily through the Bible), we won't make nature or images our idols. Instead, nature becomes evidence of His creativity. A tree becomes His living sculpture. The sky becomes His canvas and a golden-pink sunset His masterpiece, conceived in His eternal mind before He even created the moisture and energies that formed them. The exquisite orchid or the velvety petals of a rose, the fluorescent feathers of a hummingbird, and the brilliant stripes of an angelfish . . . all show us the indescribable beauty of the Master Artist Himself.

In the same way, human art can remind us of God's greatness. It need not be so-called "Christian" art. If it fits the criteria of Philippians 4:8, it will turn our spiritual eyes to the Creator with thanks and adoration—and we will see His glory.

> Whatever is true, whatever is noble, whatever is right, whatever is pure, whatever is lovely, whatever is admirable—if anything is excellent or praiseworthy—think about such things *(Philippians 4:8)*.

NINE

Can Global Oneness Save the Earth?

Both science and the teachings of Buddha tell us of the fundamental unity of all things. This understanding is crucial if we are to take positive and decisive steps on the pressing global concerns with the environment.
— The Dalai Lama, *My Tibet*[1]

I pledge allegiance to the soil ... / one ecosystem/ in diversity/ under the sun—/ With joyful interpenetration for all.
— Gary Snyder, poet[2]

The beast was given a mouth to utter proud words and blasphemies.... And he was given authority over every tribe, people, language and nation. All inhabitants of the earth will worship the beast—all whose names have not been written in the Book of Life belonging to the Lamb that was slain from the creation of the world. (Revelation 13:5-8)

LIKE OTHER COMMUNITIES around our nation, my hometown, Los Altos, publicized its list of 1990 Earth Day activities. The movie *Global Brain* caught my attention, and a few days later I watched Peter Russell's presentation of a leap-in-consciousness toward one united global mind. The movie built a "scientific" basis for this mystical hope, by "proving" that evolution occurs when organisms gather together to form larger, more complex units. Then it prophesied a final evolutionary leap into utopian harmony through the joining of human minds around the world.

The argument sounded plausible and apparently convinced many in the audience. After all, global problems demand global solutions. Earth's vanishing rainforests, spreading pollution, wasteful destruction of ocean mammals through heartless fishing practices, and careless waste disposal are just a few of the challenges that reach beyond national boundaries.

During the discussion afterward, nobody asked *who* would guide this collective global brain. Even if it were possible, what forces might such concentrated power unleash? Nor did anyone mention that this envisioned global consensus contradicts historical evidence, biblical truth, and human nature.

The Bible gives some alarming glimpses of a one-world government where the Antichrist reigns as god. In it, Satan will unleash unimaginable evils and wield absolute control over its citizens: "He also forced everyone, small and great, rich and poor, free and slave, to receive a mark on his right hand or on his forehead, so that no one could buy or sell unless he had the mark...666" *(Revelation 13:16-18)*.

Connection and Community.

"What humanity urgently needs today," said Peter Russell, "are the means to bring about a widespread shift in consciousness. This will come about, not through a revival of any particular religion, but through a revival of the techniques and experiences that once gave these teachings life and effectiveness."[3]

Revival of what techniques? Transcendental meditation, yoga, mantras, Tantric exercises?

Global education in public schools is the primary platform for this shift in consciousness. In *The New Age Masquerade* (a Christian book well worth reading), Eric Buehrer exposes the search for a "world-core curriculum" which supposedly will prepare students for a "peaceful and cooperative existence among the human species on this planet."[4]

Apparently, Dr. Gordon Cawelti, the executive director of the Association for Supervision and Curriculum Development, wants to base this world-core curriculum on a mystical book titled *New Genesis: Shaping a Global Spirituality* by Dr. Robert Muller, former under secretary of the United Nations Economic and Social Council. Let's see what Dr. Muller proposes:

The scientists have now come to the end of their wisdom. . . . This is where spirituality or religion comes in. Science in my view is part of the spiritual process; it is the transcendence and elevation of the human race into an ever vaster (sic) knowledge and consciousness of the universe and of its unfathomable, divine character.[5]

Dr. Muller envisions a world of spiritual beings evolving through reincarnation and fulfilling the law of karma—doctrines he learned from Buddhist monk U Thant, former head of the United Nations. To reach this goal, children must develop morally and spiritually through "spiritual exercises of interiority, meditation, prayer, and communion with God, the universe, and eternity."[6] (This may sound similar to Christianity, but it is the same occult *monism* that characterizes earth-based spirituality.)

Based upon their own writings, these globalists are guilty of subversion and treason. They aggressively fly in the face of public trust and push forward to indoctrinate teachers and children in their elitist, utopian dogma. They do not want to teach children *how* to think; they want to indoctrinate young minds in *what* to think.[7] (Eric Buehrer in *The New Age Masquerade*)

Muller's utopian vision matches two basic desires of people everywhere: connectedness and community. Supposedly, if people restore their ancient connections with the earth, the free flow of her mystical energies will produce a community of evolved spiritual beings who think alike and share all things. After all, if all peoples tuned their minds to a single universal brain, wouldn't they find unity?

Only if this brain were the mind of Christ. Those who are joined to Him through the cross, know His Word, and follow His leadings can enjoy genuine and unbroken oneness of mind and purpose. "We have the mind of Christ," wrote Paul. If we allow Him to be our wisdom and guide, He will build a community of caring people, "likeminded, having the same love, being one in spirit and purpose" *(1 Corinthians 2:16; Philippians 2:2).*

Those who seek oneness through counterfeit gods will eventually find the opposite: confusion instead of harmony, and hatred instead of love. The mind we follow will determine our destiny.

The Angel of Light.

There *is* a "global brain" that has spoken to people through the centuries. As always, it presents timeless deceptions fitted to the needs and desires of current listeners. Disguised as a serpent, a shining "angel of light" *(2 Corinthians 11:14),* a white light, or a dynamic human prophet, it usually offers "new" or "higher" wisdom in place of truth, human empowerment in place of God's grace, and self-realization or godhood in place of eternal life.

Since the beginning of history, this global brain has communicated through untold numbers of shamans, spiritists, gurus, and pagan priest/priestesses who, in turn, have communicated its earthy message to their followers. Where cultures demanded a more philosophical and impersonal divinity, it offered Hinduism, Buddhism, Unity, and innumerable Westernized variations of Eastern mysticism.

This global voice also speaks through people who claim loyalty to one God but who have chosen to follow a fallen angel *(Revelation 12:9)* rather than the Creator. It spoke to Muhammad back in the seventh century. The founder of Islam heard an "imperious" voice—he thought it came from the Angel Gabriel. Then "a luminous being grasped him by the throat and commanded him to repeat the sacred word."[8] Muhammad must have obeyed, for the spirit-being began to communicate a series of "revelations" which gave birth to the Quran (Koran), Islam's holy book. Along with distorted Old Testament teachings, the voice told Muhammad to rob traveling caravans, take multiple wives and concubines—his life became increasingly licentious, because "Allah willed it"—and slaughter Jews and Christians. Muhammad's Allah became a source of sheer power that inspired hatred toward God's people, commanded murder, and justified Muhammad's lusts and immorality.[9]

According to *Target Earth*, Islam is a "missionary religion"[10] meant to be taught to all people (Quran 34:28). But the Quran (9:5, 38:52) also tells Muslims to fight polytheists, Christians, and Jews—until they submit and pay tribute. Compare Islam's authoritarian reign to that of the prophesied world ruler, called the Antichrist, who will persecute God's people, and also, those who share in the Babylonian spirituality, unless they submit, bow to his image, and wear his mark (*Revelation 13:7, 15-17; 17:15-18*).

Today Muhammad's bright angel holds captive one-sixth of the world's population—precious people whom God longs to free and bless. They have pledged obedience to Allah, a god of wrath and death who couldn't care less about the destitute among his people. Just as Karma paralyzes social concern in India, so Islamic fatalism reigns in lands where "Allah willed it!" is the answer to human concerns about suffering and social injustice.

Folk Islam.

The masses who find Allah too distant and demanding to meet personal needs practice their own form of earth-based spirituality called *Folk Islam*. They have turned to a pantheon of "helpful" *powers* (spirits, fairies, dead saints, and ancestors) for protection against spells, omens, "the evil eye," and other ills caused by harmful spirits. In their mythical world, believers worship trees, stones, and angels. They communicate with spirits through dreams, visions, and divinations. They juggle occult forces through amulets, charms, magic, astrology, sorcery, and witchcraft.

Since its beginnings, Islam has been influenced by the ancient Babylonian paganism. "The fusion of animistic with the formal faith became widespread, and with it the concern for power," explains Dudley Woodberry, associate professor of Islamic studies at Fuller Theological Seminary. "The more the mix included folk elements, the greater the focus on power."[11]

Do you see the parallel to the current transformation of the West? The age-old natural drift toward earth-based power has always inspired folk religion, whether in ancient

Israel, medieval Europe or contemporary Middle East. Even when paganism seemed to disappear—as during the last three centuries in the West—a remnant lingered in superstitions, pagan myths, and fairy tales as if waiting for "an opportune time" *(Luke 4:13)*.

"It is plain that the beliefs and practices of ordinary Muslims contradict many formal aspects of Islamic faith. They ... permeate the everyday life of human beings from Morocco to Malaysia" (Bill Musk, *The Unseen Face of Islam)*.[12]

The two faces of Islam illustrate the two sides of occultism which are spreading in the West and will, in more extreme forms, dominate the end times *(Revelation 17:13)*:

☐ The earth-based spirituality of Folk Islam which offers spiritual guidance and power to manipulate at will.
☐ The dark dictatorship of orthodox Islam which demands full submission to a distorted image of God and offers little personal love, comfort or help.

An "angel" also visited Mormon founder Joseph Smith. "A romancer and diviner," Smith was no novice to occult communications. In 1822, the "angel" led him to a set of golden plates, which, as Smith tells it, he translated into English from "reformed Egyptian" with help from magic stones. According to the *Encyclopaedia Britannica,* this Book of Mormons "is regarded as a potpourri of local Indian origin legends, fragments of autobiography, and the current religious and political controversies."[13]

The point is that occult communications throughout time tend to be a blend of distorted truth and mythical repetitions fitted to the current trends. Whether people worship *one* god or many, if they don't know the God of the Bible, they are following Satan, the angel of light who is deceiving the world. (See 2 *Thessalonians 2:9-11*.) "Test the spirits," says God. "You will know them by their fruit."[14]

Chart 7, Religions of the World, shows that Satan designs a lie for everyone. People who are raised in Christian families—but without a solid scriptural foundation—can easily be led to the deceptions in column 2, which includes imitations and distortions of biblical beliefs.

Column 4 lists general forms of nature worship. Together with some variations of the force of column 5 (such as Buddhism), it shows the primary models for Deep Ecology.

Humanists are often drawn to the promise of column 5: an impersonal cosmic force available for manipulation. While it looks like monism, it also includes varying degrees of pantheism and polytheism. Contemporary pagan religions (such as witchcraft, neo-gnosticism which bears little resemblance to its old form, and Rudolf Steiner's Anthroposophy) could fit column 5 as well as 4.

Column 3 shows "the fruit" of counterfeit religions and the final bondage where people move beyond spiritual facades to total allegiance to the power of darkness. There Satan can freely exercise his hateful intent through human agents lusting after his power. Its most consistent expression is hatred for God's people—both Jews and Christians.

As you read this chart, keep in mind that only the first column represents people who remain faithful to God. All the rest demonstrate the ingenuity of the deceiver and the bait he has designed for his victims. You may want to refer back to Chart 4 which shows how earth-based religions have responded to today's call for empowered oneness and are streaming back into the post-Christian West.

Blending the World's Religions.

Breathing incense and feeling the beat of Aztec drums, my husband, Andy, and I squeezed our way through a throng of worshipers in Mexico City. The plaza outside two cathedrals dedicated to the Virgin of Guadelupe throbbed with the incessant motion of native dancers with rattles on their ankles, and the coming and going of thousands of worshipers. While most dancers wore large feathered headdresses, some (supposedly priests or medicine men) wore animal masks representing pagan empowerment. Hundreds of banners—honoring suns and snakes as well as the familiar image of the Guadalupean Virgin with the crescent moon under her feet—proclaimed loyalty to the all-too-common marriage between paganism and distorted Christianity.

It was December 12—Guadelupe Day—and Mexico was celebrating its most beloved national deity. The Virgin of

CHART 7: FIVE TYPES OF

	BIBLICAL MONOTHEISM	COUNTERFEIT MONOTHEISM Deviations/Imitations	THE POWER OF DARKNESS Satanic Manifestation
Flood	God creates God reveals Himself Noah		Rampant pre-Flood evil (Gen. 6)
	Abraham Moses	ISRAEL blends truth with PAGANISM	Black magic, sorcery Spiritism Human torture and sacrifice
1000 B.C.	David		
	Isaiah Exile ISRAEL repents –returns	ISRAEL blends truth with PAGANISM	
0	Christ Crucified	ISRAEL rejects Christ GNOSTICISM	Persecution of Jews and Christians
A.D. 500	CHURCH –Persecution	CHURCH blends truth with PAGANISM ISLAM	
	–Preservation of truth by the faithful		
1000		Church blends truth with PAGANISM	The Inquisition
1500			
1800	–Reformation		Persecution of Jews
	-Global missions -Mass media missions	JEHOVAH'S WITNESSES CHURCH blends truth with PAGANISM Wide-spread APOSTASY	Pogroms in Russia Pornography SATANISM Spreading deception

RELIGIOUS EXPRESSIONS

© 1992 Berit Kjos

POLYTHEISM/PANTHEISM/ MONISM Personified or Impersonal Deities	MONISM/PANTHEISM POLYTHEISM Impersonal Force/Divine Selves	
		Flood

PRIMITIVE NATURE-RELIGIONS
WITCHCRAFT
SUMERIAN/BABYLONIAN
  FERTILITY CULTS in Canaan,
  Egypt, India, Greece, Scandinavia . . .
HINDUISM 1500 BC
		1000 B.C.

CELTIC PAGANISM (DRUIDS)
MYSTERY RELIGIONS:
  -Eleusian: goddess Demeter
  -Phrygian: goddess Cybele and Attis.
  -Syrian and Hellenistic: Aphrodite
  -Egyptian: Isis and Osiris.
	BUDDHISM	0

	KABALA-mystical form of Judaism	A.D. 500
SHINTO (Japanese fertility cult) AMERICAN INDIANS MAYA (Central American) INCA (Peru)	SUFISM (Whirling Dervishes, -a mystical form of ISLAM)	1000
AZTEC (Mexico) EUROPEAN WITCH-CULT RELIGIONS		1500
	ROSICRUCIAN	1800

SPIRITUALISM
ANTHROPOSOPHY (Rudolf Steiner)
  founded Waldorf schools)
 	
Contemporary GODDESS-WORSHIP
  -GODDESS-PSYCHOLOGY
  -Contemporary GNOSTICISM
	MORMONISM (1823)
	BAHA'I (1843)
	THEOSOPHICAL SOCIETY (1870s)
	CHRISTIAN SCIENCE (1875)
	UNITY (1880s)
	Jung's Collective Unconscious
	SCIENTOLOGY (Dianetics)
	
	UNIFICATION CHURCH (Moonies)
	Western forms of HINDUISM
	NEW AGE Religions	

Guadelupe, titled Queen of Heaven, like Babylon's goddess Ishtar and Canaan's Asherah, had won the heart of the nation. She satisfied pagans and Catholics alike. Back in the sixteenth century, the Spanish adventurer Cortez had conquered the ancient Aztec nation and forced the proud Indians to bow to the Catholic mother of God, yet paganism continued. Mary fit right into the Aztec pantheon of gods and goddess and, in fact, became the favorite.

"Here the mother is more important than the son," explained our guide for the day. "It's different in the States."

Syncretism (fusing conflicting beliefs) is not unique to the Mexican church. It has been a natural tendency since the beginning of time. You saw Israel's shortlived faithfulness. Within a generation after the Children of Israel entered the Promised Land, they had adopted Canaanite deities. After a few centuries of life in Rome, Christians began to adopt pagan practices from their neighbors. And today many Protestant congregations are trading biblical truth for a homogenized, all-inclusive interfaith religion.

But God has always preserved a remnant. When Elijah felt alone, God reminded him that He still had 7,000 other believers who refused to worship Baal. During the Middle Ages, God preserved His Scriptures in monasteries isolated from the surrounding spiritual compromise. And in America today, in the midst of spreading apostasy, Christians from all branches of the Church are deepening their commitment to know and follow Truth.

Evangelicals are not popular among the spiritual establishment in Mexico. As always, homogenized religion opposes biblical Christianity. In fact, a blend of pagan beliefs, occult celebrations, and Bible stories in order to establish a false unity (spiritual syncretism) profanes the true God, who implores us to worship according to His guidelines and shun pagan rites:

> When you come to meet with Me, who has asked this of you, this trampling of My courts? Stop bringing meaningless offerings! Your incense is detestable to Me. New Moons, Sabbaths and convocations—I cannot bear your evil assemblies.

Depart, depart, go out from there! Touch no unclean thing! Come out from it and be pure, you who carry the vessels of the LORD *(Isaiah 1:12-13; 52:11)*.

Welcome to the Global Village.
It is not easy to resist the growing pressure to conform and assimilate. Global commerce, communication, environmental catastrophes, and the quest for a New World Order have indeed made us a global community.

National leaders who share the hope for a peaceful, environmentally sound New World Order have a single meeting ground: the United Nations. In October 1975, a gathering of religious leaders presented this statement:

> The crises of our time are challenging the world religions to release a new spiritual force transcending religious, cultural, and national boundaries into a new consciousness of the oneness of the human community and so putting into effect a spiritual dynamic toward the solutions of the world's problems.... We affirm a new spirituality ... directed toward planetary consciousness.[15]

Many of today's leaders want Christians to compromise their beliefs in order to create social consensus and spiritual oneness in the world. To educators, entertainers, ecumenists, and environmentalists who would save the earth by homogenizing all religions, separatism is heresy. Their vision of global community demands a single unifying religion or a compatible blend of inclusive religions. *Christianity doesn't fit—its exclusivity blocks the spiritual evolution toward global oneness.*

"Nonconformists are considered aberrant or deviant,"[16] says Eric Buehrer. You may have encountered that attitude if you have questioned meditation or occult influences in your child's classroom. Buehrer illustrates his point with an alarming quote from *Global Mandate* by Philip Vander Velde. Notice the transition from religious freedom to the type of religious persecution which, outside our nation, has shadowed Jews and Christians through the centuries:

Groups of the world's population should, for a long time at least, be able to choose traditional ways. . . . What alone is necessary to create a humane world society is that all subcultures be . . . compatible with the world society's view of itself and of nature, and compatible with the unity of humanity and the earth. *To the extent that any cultural tendency denied this, it would be aberrant; to the extent that such a tendency was expressed in action, it would be subversive; and to the extent that such a tendency might become powerful, it would be fought.* (emphasis added)[17]

Signs of growing persecution are darkening the Western World. To enforce consensus and create "a culturally inclusive environment," environmentalists and other visionaries are replacing our Judeo-Christian values with those that produce decadence and tyranny. Look at how the Western World promotes pagan values while it outlaws expressions of moral boundaries:

☐ A government report blames Christianity for causing teenage suicides. Published in 1989 by the *U.S. Department of Health and Human Services,* it accused Catholics, Baptists, and other Christian groups of depicting homosexuality as morally wrong, thus creating "unresolvable internal conflicts for youth who adhere to their faith but believe they will not change their sexual orientation." The recommendation: churches must change their beliefs. "Religion needs to reassess homosexuality in a positive context . . . "[18]

☐ The Hate Crimes bill requires the Justice Department to keep statistics on "crimes" motivated by hatred based on race, religion, ethnicity or sexual orientation. Somehow, it is supposed to abolish prejudice, yet, it is used against those who violate "politically correct thinking." In Sweden, an evangelical pastor served a four-week jail sentence for violating a Swedish anti-hate statute which protects homosexuals and other groups from embarrassing "verbal violence." He had preached a sermon about Sodom, Gomorrah, and the biblical consequences for disobedience.[19]

☐ "A conservative student newspaper at the State University of New York at Birmingham editorialized against the creation of a Department of Gay and Lesbian Studies. The paper's funds were cut off, and the editors were forced to attend a sensitivity training session"—a new form of mental manipulation or brainwashing to impose consensus: "stomp out disagreement with the left-liberal mind-set."[20]

You have probably noticed the growing public hostility toward those who object to classroom curricula that use occult formulas or emphasize violence or occult themes, such as appear in some of the *Impressions* reading series. Caring parents who express their concern are labeled closed-minded, anti-intellectual, myopic, fundamentalist, censors. Emotion rather than reason set the tone. Educators determined to pursue their chosen path to "social reform" often block communication, and exclude, insult, or reject Christian parents.

The war against God in this country, specifically against Jesus Christ, is getting uglier, much uglier, much more explicit. And make no mistake about it, please. This war is against Christ.[21] (John Lofton, syndicated Washington columnist)

WHAT CAN FAMILIES DO?

☐ Pray and faithfully read the Bible together.
☐ Know and discuss ...
  1. How to build God's kind of global community.
  2. How to face persecution.
  3. The God who reigns.
☐ Choose a family project from pages 170–175.

1. HOW TO BUILD GOD'S KIND OF GLOBAL COMMUNITY. God created us for fellowship with Himself, and He longs to pour out His love and blessings on a world that will receive Him. "Go into all the world and make disciples,"[22] He commissions His people. Most of us don't have

to go far. The world's people have become our neighbors. Like the rest of us, they face loneliness, pain, and disappointments. We can invite them into our homes, learn to understand, but not adopt, their ways, discover our similarities, and show them God's love.

The environmental crisis has opened new doors. As we work side by side to clean our neighborhood, we can teach respect for God's creation—and be ready to point people to the Creator. He will provide opportunities—if we make ourselves available to Him.

We will face opposition and competition. God's Word shows us that at "the end of the age," apostasy and the Gospel will spread side by side throughout the world. It is happening. People everywhere are searching for spiritual reality. Buddhist study centers are multiplying in Western nations, while about twenty-four million Japanese (twenty percent of Japan's population) have flocked to "new" religions.[23] Even as Bibles pour into Russia and teachers learn to share biblical truth with their students, "the Soviets are rediscovering a host of fantastic philosophers, free-thinking mystics, and offbeat occultists."[24] The spiritually starved masses are grabbing anything that offers answers: New Age mysticism, Buddhism, Hinduism, Islam, Mormonism—along with enticing blends of everything. While militant Hindus are determined to purge India of all other religions—especially Christianity, ex-guru Rabi Maharaj travels around the world as an ambassador for Jesus. He described a 1990 visit to Eastern Europe in his newsletter:

> The cults and sects, both Eastern and Western, are having a heyday. Moonies are establishing schools teaching English in order to win followers. The New Age is growing rapidly. I saw Hare Krishna disciples in every city I visited. . . . And Czechoslovakian President Havel meditated publicly with the Dalai Lama of Tibet, openly endorsing Eastern religions. . . . In fact, the official former Communist headquarters in Bratislava has been turned over to New Agers.[25]

This is no time to sit on the sidelines or to be afraid. As

soldiers of the King, we fight on the winning side. Jesus told His disciples, "As long as it is day, we must do the work of Him who sent Me. Night is coming, when no one can work" *(John 9:4)*. This work is to allow Him to live His life through us, so that His transforming love can touch the hurting multitudes and draw them into His gentle embrace. Remember, "Salvation is found in no one else, for there is no other name under heaven given to men by which we must be saved" *(Acts 4:12)*.

3. HOW TO FACE PERSECUTION. The above truth invites hatred. Only by wearing the armor and wielding its "sword of the Spirit, which is the Word of God," can we resist the world's arguments against us. Because of our beliefs, we are accused of being . . .

☐ Judgmental: People say, "You criticize our way—you don't think we're good enough for God!" *(Romans 3:23-24)*
☐ Arrogant: "You think you're better than us—that you have found the only way to eternal life!" *(John 14:6)*
☐ Narrow-minded: "You think you have the only handle on truth. If you practiced the love you preach, you would see all people as worthy of salvation" *(1 Timothy 4:1)*.
☐ Ignorant: "You simply don't know the other paths to enlightenment" *(2 Timothy 4:3-4)*.
☐ Old-Fashioned: "You cling to obsolete myths" *(Hebrews 13:8)*.

For the message of the cross is foolishness to those who are perishing, but to those who are being saved it is the power of God. *(1 Corinthians 1:18)*

Could we really be persecuted for our faith in the United States? After all, the Bill of Rights guarantees our religious liberty. Centuries of freedom to worship God and express His truth have taught us to take these rights for granted.

We forget that *committed* Jews and Christians around the world have almost always been despised and oppressed, often by an established church that had compromised its faith and then refused to be confronted by truth. America was settled and founded by Christian immigrants who fled religious persecution. In the turbulent history of the world, America's period of religious freedom has been like a restful oasis—a contradiction to the norm.

I used to wonder at Jesus' words in John 15:18-21. They didn't seem relevant to the American Christian. Now I read them with new understanding:

> If the world hates you, keep in mind that it hated Me first. If you belonged to the world, it would love you as its own. As it is, you do not belong to the world, but I have chosen you out of the world. That is why the world hates you. Remember the words I spoke to you: "No servant is greater than his master." If they persecuted Me, they will persecute you also . . . for they do not know the One who sent Me.

Those who reject Jesus will shun us, for faithful believers carry the presence of the Holy Spirit who brings conviction of sin as well as God's love. Any mention of *sin* grates against today's relativistic values and the kind of "freedom" where anything goes. That's why we, who are "the aroma of Christ" to believers, are also "the smell of death to those who are perishing." They hate the true Jesus. "But thanks be to God, who always leads us in His triumph" (2 *Corinthians* 2:14-15, NASB).

We are "more than conquerors" because Jesus is in and with us. He wants us to know Him as our caring Shepherd who goes before us, our strong Refuge where we can hide, our unfailing Hope—who, unlike the world's pie-in-the-sky-hope will accomplish all He has promised.

Our King calls us to share His suffering, misunderstanding, rejection, and loneliness—to be counted as fools for His sake. Are we ready? We must stay close together, rejoicing in the overcoming power of the One true God who is far greater than His enemy. By Jesus' strength in us, we are able to stand firm in one spirit, contending as one man for the faith of the Gospel without being frightened in any way

> Blessed are you when men hate you, when they exclude you
> and insult you and reject your name as evil, because of the
> Son of Man. Rejoice in that day and leap for joy, because great
> is your reward in heaven. *(Luke 6:22-23)*

by those who oppose [us]" *(Philippians 1:27-28).*

4. THE GOD WHO REIGNS. Memorize biblical promises
of victory: Exodus 14:13-14, 23:20-22; Deuteronomy 31:6;
Joshua 1:9; 2 Chronicles 20:15, 17, 22; 1 Corinthians 15:57;
Romans 8:37. Remember, these Scripture swords are the
offensive part of your armor. Affirm them whenever you
face spiritual battles, and you will experience the triumph of
the God who reigns.

Nothing is more exciting than watching God win His
battles—especially when He lets us participate. During the
fall of 1990 I shared in one such victory.

Reading the newspaper one morning, I noticed that the
Dalai Lama, god-king of Tibetan Buddhists, would sweep
through the Bay Area during the second week of October.
For two full days, the gentle Nobel Peace Prize winner
would teach meditation, chanting, and "empowerment" rituals at the San Jose State University arena. On October 10,
he would descend via helicopter on Mount Tamalpais to
"invoke the spirits of this area" and to receive "the blessings
of enlightened spiritual masters" such as the Lord Buddha,
Jesus Christ, and Muhammad in a healing and peace ceremony. The same afternoon, he would bring his inspirational
guidance into Grace Cathedral, where the Buddhist master
and the city's religious leaders would make a joint commitment to pursue world peace.

The article made occultism seem so normal—and so healing! My heart ached as I prayed, "Lord, how can the Dalai
Lama, who represents faith in yoga, reincarnation, tantric
rituals and cosmic oneness, lead worship in a cathedral built
to honor You?"

To those ignorant of the invisible war raging around us,
the news must have sounded good. Who wouldn't want

healing, harmony, empowerment, and peace? I felt almost guilty for questioning ideals that warm the hearts of all—Christians as well as pantheists and monists. Didn't God call us to oneness with Himself and each other? *Yes, but we become one only when we are joined to Christ at the cross.*

One with Jesus, we have something special to offer others: His life. But Christ's life is totally incompatible with a religion linked to tantric yoga, enlightened gods, and demonic spirits—even when it comes cloaked in enticing terms such as unity and environmental healing.

Now these forces had been invited into God's house. "My Lord," I prayed, "What can I do? Attend the meeting and pray against the powers of darkness? Immediately a Scripture flashed through my mind: "Now go; I will help you speak and will teach you what to say" (*Exodus 4:12*).

"Are You speaking to me, Lord? I need confirmation." I waited. My thoughts turned to King Jehoshaphat's triumph in 2 Chronicles 20:17. God quenched the power of the enemy when His people praised Him and followed His directions: "Take your positions; stand firm and see the deliverance the Lord will give you. . . . Do not be discouraged. Go out to face them tomorrow, and the Lord will be with you."

On the morning of the 10th, I drove into San Francisco. When I arrived at the Episcopal cathedral, others were already waiting. A delightful young woman introduced herself. When she told me that she was Buddhist, I asked her to help me understand her beliefs. She began by explaining that Buddhism has many forms: Soto Zen, Rinsai, Tibetan, Korean. . . . She herself observed the Japanese version. Having rejected the reality of God, heaven and hell, she believed in "the Eternal" within each person.

The crush of admirers streaming into the cathedral testified to the success of Buddhist evangelism. By early afternoon, all public rows were filled. Even the latecomers' frustration with the lack of seating couldn't quench the rising anticipation.

Meanwhile, I kept praying that Jesus Christ, who had put Satan in submission under His feet (*Ephesians 1:20-23*) and "disarmed [Satan's] rulers and authorities" (*Colossians 2:15*) would crush the enemy's power in this place. That, as in

Elijah's days, all counterfeit gods would be proven ineffective. That there would be no alliance made between God's followers and those of false gods. I sensed a fellowship with other Christians—either in the assembly or at home—who were battling with me in prayer.

Ushers passed out invitations to next month's "rarely performed Buddhist Medicine Empowerment Ceremony . . . to tap the power of our imagination to heal . . . culminating in the activation of unconscious and powerful levels of the psyche. . . . The monks will close by blessing and harmonizing the environment to insure and evoke the presence of enlightened teachers [ascended spirit entities] and healers . . . " I prayed that God would block these demonic forces.

At 3 P.M. the Dalai Lama's scheduled arrival—heads turned back toward the large doors, waiting. At 3:20 we were still waiting. And at 3:45, creaking benches and impatient voices suggested that people grew weary of waiting. Finally, an hour late, the Tibetan trumpets blew and the doors swung open. Enveloped in a smoky cloud of juniper incense—believed to purify the environment and heal relationships—the procession of spiritual leaders marched up the aisle. All except the Dalai Lama. Our eyes continued to guard the back doors.

A voice from the podium spoke. "Unfortunately the Dalai Lama is indisposed." The unwelcome words crushed all hope. In the midst of confused whispers and a few hurried departures, the ceremony proceeded with the prayers of the various church leaders positioned around the altar. But the sound system didn't work. From all parts of the room came shouts of "We can't hear!" But nobody solved the problem.

Walking out after the aborted ceremony, I noticed a woman crying. "Are you all right?" I asked. She didn't answer. "Would you like to talk or would you rather be alone?" I didn't want to intrude.

"I'm so disappointed," she burst out. "This was such a failure. I couldn't even hear what they said."

"It was confusing, wasn't it? How could the Dalai Lama be disabled after the healing ceremony this morning?"

Sadness filled her voice as she answered. "I don't understand. It sounded so perfect. All the religions joining together. Why did everything go wrong?"

Seeking life-giving answers, I prayed. Suddenly thoughts began to flow. I said, "Maybe God doesn't like our attempts to control the world and seek oneness apart from Him."

"Why wouldn't He want us to get together and make the world more peaceful?"

"Maybe He knows our plans wouldn't work. That by trusting ourselves and magical powers rather than Him, we would lose sight of the only real hope we have."

"But the Dalai Lama trusts God. His monks just came from the Vatican where they talked with the Pope and his monks about unity and meditation."

"I wonder what kind of unity Christians can enjoy with Buddhists without compromising their faith. Christianity is God-centered and Buddhism is self-centered." I waited a moment before continuing. "I don't dare rely on myself anymore. It is so much easier to admit my weaknesses and trust the only One who can give me the strength and wisdom I need—Jesus Christ. He says to you and me, "My peace I give you. I do not give to you as the world gives. Do not let your hearts be troubled" *(John 14:27).*

We talked a long time. Her futile search for peace had led her on and off numerous spiritual paths. Now, in her frustration, she was ready to listen to the only One who could love, shepherd, and fulfill her. I gave her a little book about Him, and we agreed to meet again soon.

All the way home I praised my Lord, who once again had proven Himself the sovereign, omnipotent King of Kings. Our God reigns!

TEN

This Is Our Father's World—
a Christian View of Ecology

Dean A. Ohlman
President, Christian Nature Federation

This is my Father's world, and to my listening ears
All nature sings, and round me rings the music of the
spheres.
This is my Father's world: I rest me in the thought
Of rocks and trees, of skies and seas—His hand the wonders
wrought.

LIKE BERIT, I have studied the New Age Movement and its philosophies for several years. I too have become alarmed at the way the once casual and spiritually neutral term, *mother earth*, has been laden with neopagan implications. Equally alarming is the manner in which this new meaning has gained acceptance by thousands of individuals who are members and supporters of various nature and environmental action groups.

That the granddaddy of environmental action agencies, the Sierra Club, would publish a source book recommending our communicating with the "spirit of the earth" (*Well Body, Well Earth*) is cause for Christians to be on the alert for satanic deception in the environmental movement. At the same time, however, it should compel us to ask the question, "If people are once again looking for the spiritual significance in our earthly existence, why are they turning to pantheism and other pagan theologies instead of Christianity?" Is there something missing in the daily demonstration of our faith that sends them looking elsewhere for spiritual meaning, or are they merely refusing to accept God's conditions for spiritual salvation? I believe it is a bit of both.

In particular, let's examine the stumbling blocks Christians sometimes unwittingly place in the way of spiritual seekers. The following beliefs are generally considered to be true by most believers, but they can be voiced and acted on in a manner that draws or drives away those who would like to consider the claims of Christ.

This Earth Is Not Our Home.

Paul in his epistle to the Philippians says about the enemies of the cross that "their mind is on earthly things." Of believers he says, "But our citizenship is in heaven. And we eagerly await a Savior from there, the Lord Jesus Christ" *(Philippians 3:19-20)*. To emphasize this belief, we sing the words of as popular chorus: "This world is not my home, I'm just a passin' through."

The truth is relatively simple: For the Christian, the earth is now a temporary dwelling place for the corruptible earthly body. When the Lord returns, our spirits will occupy incorruptible heavenly bodies and dwell in the new heaven or the new earth. We call this our "blessed hope."

However, the truth also remains that right now this temporary earth is as much our collective home as our earthly bodies are the temporary individual residences of our spirit. And just as much as God has given us guidelines on how we occupy our bodies, he has given us mandates regarding our occupation of the physical earth. Furthermore, both the earth and our bodies were created by God and must not be despised. Indeed, our bodies are the temples of the Holy Spirit who resides with us on earth.

Christians often point to the error of the Hindu who practices yoga in order to become spiritually detached from the *maya* (illusion) of his physical existence; yet we are quick to deny the claims of non-Christians that we, too, frequently consider the physical world to be of little importance. They point out that our beliefs about our future existence in heaven make us insensitive to the problems surrounding us on earth. To them we seem to be saying, "There's no sense in our giving attention to the earth's environmental problems; we're not going to live here long anyway."

Fans of "Star Trek" are accustomed to hearing their heroes who are caught in distressing circumstances paging the *Enterprise* with the words, "Beam me up, Scotty!" And in an instant they are dematerialized out of trouble and rematerialized in the safety of the spaceship. The relationship of this fantasy to the reality of the Christian's blessed hope has inspired some believers to change the trekker's distress call to "Beam me up, Lord!" Is it any wonder that non-Christians seeing this on our bumper stickers come to the conclusion that all Christians want to do about the earth's environmental problems is to escape?

The Bible, of course, does not give us any hint of a possible "on demand" escape from the earth's condition. In fact, we are given a mandate from God to be stewards of His creation handiwork. God gives us no excuse for neglecting or despoiling the earth. Until Jesus comes, he expects us "to work it and take care of it" *(Genesis 2:15)*. The broad meaning of the Hebrew terms for *work it* and *take care of it* is "to dress, serve, till, and tend it and to keep, protect, observe, and save it." Therefore, it is not un-Christian to speak of "saving" the earth.

So long as we dwell in our earthly bodies, the physical earth is our home, and we are responsible to care for it as good stewards. Let's not place a stumbling block before unbelievers by ignoring our stewardship responsibilities.

The Earth Is Wearing Out.

The psalmist says, and the writer of Hebrews repeats, that the earth will wear out "like a garment" *(Psalm 102:26)*. And Paul tells the Romans that "the creation itself will be liberated from its bondage to decay" at the time when our bodies will be redeemed *(Romans 8:21)*.

Though Christians may differ on how they believe the earth will be renewed or replaced, they agree that this earth is now decaying. Therefore, it is easy to look upon the present environmental conditions as proof of this process. In fact, that is likely the case. However, acknowledging that the earth is wearing out is not the same as believing we should hasten the process or shrug our shoulders and declare that we can't do anything about it. We all know that our earthly bodies are also wearing out, but we usually do all we can to slow the aging process and give them tender loving care as long as we have them.

Nowhere in Scripture is it indicated that because the earth is aging, we can neglect our earthkeeping tasks. We do not know God's timetable, and it may be, in His great mercy and grace, that the return of Christ is centuries away. It is obvious that the earth has a great deal of life left in it if we do not foolishly squander its resources. In fact, the Bible has many warnings for those who would despoil the land.

We must not use the fact that the earth is predictably wearing out as an excuse to neglect God's mandate to "take care of it," a phrase that can also mean "to preserve it." Such an attitude is indeed a stumbling block for spiritual seekers who should expect Christians, of all people, to show care and concern for God's creation gift to us.

God Gave People Dominion over the Earth and Told Us to Subdue It.

Probably no other aspect of the Genesis mandate has been more misunderstood than the dominion aspect. It has been misunderstood or misapplied by both believers and unbelievers. The reason for such misunderstanding is a common one: the failure to interpret the meaning of one part of God's Word in the light of the rest of Scripture.

Although the Hebrew terms for "dominion" and "subdue" can have negative meanings implying ruthlessness, they also refer to reigning over or bringing into subjection—like a governor ruling over his people or a horseman over his mount. It is obvious from the rest of God's Word that the Creator did not grant to mankind the freedom to run roughshod over the earth like a ravaging army. One cannot abuse the earth and at the same time "work it" and take care of it." These tasks when taken together describe the responsibilities of a steward. And Francis Schaeffer reminded us that this dominion of mankind over the other living things is under God's dominion and in God's domain.

If nothing else, having dominion over any of God's creation should make us both humble and diligent. It was the entrance of sin that led mankind to the pride, envy, and carelessness that have had such a devastating impact on the earth. And in our relationships with unbelievers we must demonstrate that we have been freed from the bondage of sin that would make us spoilers of the earth. It is to our shame that secular environmentalists are quicker than Christians in pointing out the evils of uncontrolled materialism.

One of the problems of conservative Christians identifying with conservative politics, capitalism, and a free-market economy is that we often tend to sanctify consumerism. We are prone to believe that every time an environmentalist suggests we alter our lifestyles to become less consumption oriented, it is tantamount to treason and un-American.

This is unfortunate, for it could very easily be demonstrated from Scripture that most of us are living extravagant lifestyles that thrive on covetousness and that for the most part we are ignoring Jesus' instruction about not laying up treasures on earth. It is likely that truly living like a Christian might actually be "un-American." Environmental philosophers have pointed out that if all Americans lived by the Golden Rule, our economic system would collapse overnight.

The principles of Christian stewardship should motivate us to reexamine how we are using the resources God gave to us—how we are doing in our dominion tasks. Consider the fact given to us by Dr. James Bowyer of the University of Minnesota that we burn 10 million tons of coal a year just to heat our waterbeds. Bowyer asks, "Where is it written that we should have waterbeds and that they should be heated?" When you add up the monetary cost of extracting that coal, transporting it, and turning it into electricity and the resulting degradation of the environment, one has to wonder if Jesus would have a heated waterbed if He were living in America today. Do we dare even ask such questions?

People Are the Most Valuable of God's Creations on Earth.
This is in one of the most offensive Christian beliefs to many secular environmentalists, in particular to those who

consider themselves to be "deep ecologists." Deep ecologists believe that anthropocentrism (believing that everything revolves around mankind) is a curse on the earth. Their belief is that since everything on earth is connected and interdependent, no one element is more valuable than another,.

Christianity, however, declares that people are more valuable than other created things. This belief in part comes from Jesus' statement in His Sermon on the Mount that people are "much more valuable" than birds (*Matthew 6:26*). Other scriptural truths apply: that God sacrificed His Son for people, that people are the particular objects of God's love, that people were alone created in God's image, that people are to rule over the works of His hand, and that people are in a position only a little lower than the angels (*Psalm 8:5-6*).

Deep ecologists to the contrary, there is no denying the anthropocentricity of mankind in creation. However, such centrality does not mean that all things on earth have value only as they apply to mankind and his needs and wants. God declared all things good even before man was created. In the Revelation, John further clarified the issue: "Thou art worthy, O Lord, to receive glory and honor and power; for Thou hast created all things, and for Thy pleasure they are and were created" (*4:11*).

If we recognize that it was for God's pleasure all things were created, we must understand that our being in a central position is not cause for pride, but for great humility because we can carry out the responsibilities of such a position only with God's power and wisdom working through us. When sin entered the world, arrogant people took their honored position and abused it—acting as though they themselves were God. The environmental damage we see around us is not the result of our position, but the result of our sin and the abuse of our position.

This being the case, Christians should be models before the world of what it means to have proper rule over the remainder of God's creation. In fact, a good case could be made for the argument that this planet's environmental condition will not improve until Christians start acting as Christians should regarding the use of the earth. Unless we are arrogant enough to believe that only what pleases man pleases God, we had better think again about how we tread upon this hallowed ground. Dare we see all forests as timber, all prairies as crop land, all mountains of coal as fuel, and all lesser creatures as food or subjects for sport?

Evangelism Is More Important Than Earth Stewardship. If we Christians are to correctly answer our Lord's question, "What shall it profit a man, if he shall gain the whole world, and lose his own soul?" we must recognize the priority of the soul over the body. It would indeed be foolish for us to protest our community's air pollution and ignore the spiritual condition of our next door neighbor. What good is it if a man breathes pure air to live ten years longer and still loses his own soul?

Knowing this about Christianity, it should be easy for the unbeliever to understand why Christians find it immoral for the government to spend hundreds of thousands of dollars to save stranded whales, yet treat the fetal body of the human soul as trash for the dumpster.

Nonetheless, this does not give the Christian an excuse to ignore the stewardship mandate. The Christian life is a life of balance, and caring for the creation is a part of that life. God has given us many responsibilities in many different areas of our lives, and we cannot ignore those things that we have chosen to place lower on our priority list. We know from Scripture that partial obedience is really not an option for Christians.

The Conclusions of Scientists Often Conflict with Christian Beliefs about the Earth.

No doubt one of the major difficulties Christians have with secular environmentalists is that their theories and conclusions never acknowledge God as we know Him (although they sometimes refer to a First Cause or to Gaia, the earth Goddess), nor do they recognize the authority of God's Word. There is never any suggestion that God is sovereign over the earth and that it will not be destroyed by the hand of man. Neither is there any acknowledgment that God created all things, and that people are special because they are created in God's image. The secular doomsday conclusions about the fate of the earth make it appear that only mankind can keep the earth from dying. And all of this is couched in Darwinian terms regarding the threat to our "evolutionary development."

Because of this, Christians are quick to pick up on the fact that there is a great deal of controversy about such things as global warming, overpopulation, ozone depletion, acid rain, and a number of other theories regarding the condition of the earth. Animal rights activists are looked upon as pantheists or secular humanists who do acknowledge the special nature of man. Protestors of rain forest destruction are considered to be Hinduistic vegetarians or Darwinists alarmed about the threat to our evolutionary advancement. And those who express concern about pollution, waste, overdependence upon foreign oil, and the depletion of natural resources are often considered to be sentimentalists who expect the earth to last forever and desire "pristine" conditions to remind them of the past.

Unfortunately, all of these are oversimplified conclusions that ignore a great deal of scriptural instruction and admonition. First of all, it should not be necessary to "prove" a dire, earth-threatening cataclysm to convince us that pollution and waste are not aspects of good stewardship. Christians should desire clean air, pure water, and healthy soil as essential to our earthkeeping responsibilities. And although God gave Noah and his descendants the right to eat the meat of animals, one has to go a long way to conclude from that fact that people have the absolute right to use and abuse animals any way they wish. In fact, there are a number of passages in Scripture that call for kind and humane treatment of animals.

Furthermore, it is also clear from Scripture that even God's people are not immune from the law of sowing and reaping. What arrogance it is for us to assume that we can lay waste the earth and not suffer dire consequences. God seldom withholds the consequences of mankind defying the natural laws He has established; and perhaps, more important, He usually lets us on earth suffer the consequences of defying His moral laws—even though in Christ we are forgiven and will eventually inherit eternal life.

The conclusion here is this: although we must be alert to the manner in which Satan is using the environmental movement for his own purposes, we must not neglect our continuing stewardship responsibilities regarding the earth. By such neglect, Christians are missing a great opportunity to be witnesses before the people of the world of what it means to honor and praise God for His wonderful creation gifts to us. Indeed, how can we not expect people to turn to false gods like the earth Goddess if we do not ourselves live in obedience to the one true God as faithful tenders of the earth?

This chapter began with the first verse of Maltbie Babcock's anthem "This Is My Father's World." The words to this hymn first appeared as a poem in Babcock's collection *Thoughts for Every Day Living*. As you read the final two verses, you might pledge to make these your everyday thoughts; for there is no better encouragement than the spirit-lifting truth that "though the wrong seems oft so strong, God is the Ruler yet." How thrilling is the fact that our faith is not in a mystical earth Goddess, but in a personal, loving Heavenly Father.

> *This is my Father's world, the birds their carols raise,*
> *The morning light, the lily white, declare their Maker's praise.*
> *This is my Father's world: He shines in all that's fair;*
> *In the rustling grass I hear Him pass; He speaks to me everywhere.*
>
> *This is my Father's world, O let me ne'er forget*
> *That though the wrong seems oft so strong, God is the Ruler yet.*
> *This is my Father's world: The battle is not done;*
> *Jesus who died shall be satisfied, and earth and heaven be one.*

Family Projects
and Helpful Resources

1. *ENJOY GOD'S CREATION.* Spend a day outside in a park or forest near you. You may want to bring along . . .

☐ *A magnifying glass* to watch a tiny insect crawl up a leaf, to examine the details of a lost feather, or to see what kinds of life hide in tree bark or rocks.

☐ *Binoculars* to get close-up views of squirrels, birds, and nests.

☐ *A compass* to show you the direction you walk.

☐ *Old plastic bags.* Use them to sit on and to collect litter dropped along the path. You please God when you make His creation more beautiful.

☐ *A guide book* to help you learn the names of plants and animals. A fun book to take on a hike is *Crinkelroot's Guide to Walking in Wild Places* by naturalist Jim Arnosky.

2. *MAKE A FIVE-MINUTE BIRDFEEDER.* The EarthWorks Group share some great ideas in their book called, *50 Simple Things Kids Can Do to Save the Earth.* Here are two suggestions for feeding hungry birds:

☐ Tie some unsalted peanuts (still in their shells) on a piece of yarn or string. Hang from a branch.

☐ Spread peanut butter into the grooves of a pine cone. Hang outside.

☐ Some birds also like orange peel. Hang some funny shapes in a tree.

☐ Best of all, grow bird food in your yard. (Of course, that will take a lot longer than five minutes.) A free booklet,

"Invite Birds into Your Home," suggests many ways you can make birds feel at home in your yard. Order it from Soil Conservation Service, Room 0054-S, P.O. Box 2890, Washington, D.C. 20013.

3. *SAVE PAPER—AND TREES.* Make your own *reusable* lunchbag. Instead of using *ordinary* paper lunch bags, sew a special one out of corduroy, denim, or any other strong washable fabric. Close it with strips of Velcro. Decorate it with iron-on patches or fabric paint. Embroider or paint your name.

You can find specific instructions in the *Earthbook for Kids* by Linda Schwartz.

4. *RECYCLE—AND BUY RECYCLED PRODUCTS.* Save trees, energy, and other resources by recycling paper, aluminum cans, and glass. (Leave out broken mirrors, plate glass, and lightbulbs. Their special coating doesn't recycle.)

Most of us buy recycled glass without even knowing it, but we often have to go out of our way to get recycled paper. I order stationery, gift wrap, note pads, and toilet paper from *Earth Care Paper Inc.* P.O. Box 7070, Madison, WI 53707. Call 608-277-2900 for a free catalog.

Remember, if we don't buy recycled paper products, the stockpiles of used newspapers will simply be dumped into landfills.

For more information, read *The Recycler's Handbook* by the EarthWorks Group.

5. *DO YOUR OWN COMPOSTING.* You can turn your fruit, vegetable, and yard wastes into nutrient-rich soil. Just let it decompose (break down) naturally. You can buy a composter for about a $100 (see Seventh Generation catalog below), but you don't need it. Simply dig a pit in your yard, then layer the following:

☐ Kitchen wastes such as thin-sliced orange peels and vegetable scraps.

☐ Yard wastes such as small sticks, grass (in thin layers) and leaves (which supply oxygen).

☐ The soil you dug up. When you cover food scraps with

grass and soil, they won't attract flies.

☐ If you want to see what happens to *non-biodegradable* items when they are tossed somewhere in nature, add a pen or a plastic bag. Do they change?

Keep the composting pit moist until ready for use—about four to six months. While you wait, you may want to start a second pit. For more information order a $3 guide, "The Simple Art of Home Composting," from Ecology Action, P.O. Box 1188, Santa Cruz, CA 95061.

6. *WAYS TO SAVE ENERGY.* Everything we do uses energy. Centuries ago, most people only used human and animal energy. They would walk or ride a horse rather than drive.

Do we really need all the power we use? Look around your home and see how many appliances and gadgets you have today that your great-grandparents did without. How could you get the same work done without those appliances? Make lists and compare them. See who in your family (1) made the longest list, (2) had the best ideas. Try them out.

We all need to work together to save energy. It is easy for us to plug in a toaster, but the power that heats it is not as cheap as it seems. All our ways to generate electricity have hidden costs:

☐ *Fossil fuels* (coal, oil, natural gas), our most common sources of energy, pollute and are non-renewable. Unlike the sun and wind, they can't be used again. Unlike plants, they don't grow back.

☐ *Water* is renewable, but generating hydropower usually means building a huge dam and transforming a natural river valley into an artificial lake.

☐ *Nuclear energy* produces radioactive waste along with electric power. Disposing of this toxic waste is a serious problem.

☐ *Solar energy* as a source of electricity takes up large amounts of land. Producing the high-tech parts for heating fluid, generating steam, and producing electricity is often polluting.

☐ *Light energy* (photovoltaics) converts the sun's energy directly into usable power. Light changes to electricity when it hits the solid-state cell. But producing these solar cells is still both expensive and polluting.

☐ *Wind power* works well when the winds blow faster than 12 miles per hour. But people have complained that the windmills on California hilltops mar the landscape and kill birds.

☐ *Tidal force* is another potential power source, but how would you like to see a power plant on the coast nearest you?

As the population grows, we will need more energy. We may have to use all of the above. Still, the best way to help care for God's creation is to avoid wasting any of it.

One way to cut down on electricity is to use high efficiency lamps and bulbs. If your local stores don't stock them, suggest that they do. Meanwhile, you can order them from Eco Source (Call 1-800-688-8345 for a free catalog) or *The Energy Federation*, 354B Waverly St., Farmingham, MA 01701.

7. *MAKE A SOLAR OVEN—AND USE IT.* A solar oven (or box cooker) is an insulated box that captures enough of the sun's heat to bake food. It can be made from cardboard (or wood) and glass in one afternoon.

You can order plans for "Your Own Solar Box" for $5 from *Solar Box Cookers International*, 1724 11th Street, Sacramento, CA 95814.

8. *HELP SAVE THE RAINFOREST.* Tropical rainforests form a dense band of trees along parts of the equator. They are home to countless plants and animals not found anywhere else.

Today, these rich forests are being cut down at an alarming rate. Some say that 40 to 50 percent of the world's rainforests have already been destroyed, while 5 to 15 percent of the Amazon forests have been cleared.

Some of the trees are cut to make paper and wood products (rosewood, teak, ebony) much of which is sold to the United States and other nations. Other parts of the forests are burned to clear the land for farming and cattle grazing. Without the trees, the rain soon washes away the nutrients in the thin topsoil. The sun then bakes the ground into a brick-hard surface.

You can help people earn a living without cutting trees by buying the fruit and nuts that grow in the forest. Simply . . .

☐ Buy Ben and Jerry's RainForest Crunch ice cream.

☐ Order Brazil nuts, cashews, dried fruit, and other forest products from *Seventh Generation*, Colchester, VT 05446-1672. Call 1-800-456-1197 for free catalog.

9. *VALUE WATER ENOUGH TO CONSERVE.* Thousands of people around the world are dying because of famines caused by too little rain. In our land of abundance, we can hardly imagine such suffering. We usually take our water for granted. I did—until California was hit by a drought. Now my family is *really* grateful for water! In fact, we enjoy the challenge of finding new ways to conserve. Here are some of them:

☐ Look for drippy faucets. To see how fast the drips add up, put a bucket under the faucet and let it fill up. Then give the water to thirsty plants.

☐ Keep a bucket in your shower. Save the cold water you usually waste while waiting for warm water. Use it to water plants or fill up the tank behind the toilet when you flush. (You can also save water by filling a plastic bag or bottle with water and keeping it in the tank.)

☐ Use low-flow faucets and shower heads.

☐ Thank God for the water He provides. In Old Testament days, His people considered it one of His most precious gifts.

10. *PRAY FOR THE WORLD'S HUNGRY PEOPLE.* Ask God to show them His love in special ways (maybe He will use you) so that they will want to know Him.

☐ To help you understand their struggles and needs, read and discuss the wonderful Christian atlas *Target Earth* edited by Frank Kaleb Jansen. It is full of colorful charts and fascinating information about the people of the world. For example, it tells us that 24,000 children die daily from diseases such as typhus, cholera, and dysentery because they drink polluted, untreated water. We can make a difference by praying (1) that they turn to the only One who can end droughts and provide needed rain and (2) that He send people who can help them replace polluted streams with safe, clean water.

Target Earth also tells about 2.2 billion people (speaking over 5,000 languages) who have never heard about our God. Ask God to send them missionaries with the good news about the love of Jesus Christ. The "Stories of Hope" section shows what happens when God's love touches hurting lives.

Environmental Organizations and Literature

"Saving the earth has never seemed so important, or so confusing," wrote Bill Gifford and the editors of *Outside* magazine. In their 1990 article, "Inside the Environmental Groups," they describe and evaluated the twenty-five largest (according to membership) environmental groups in the nation. The following chart is based on more recent data. All the information—except the last column—was approved in 1991 by the respective organizations.

Gifford's "Milquetoast/Bombthrower Index" (MB column) rates each group according to its dealings with "the establishment" (Congress, courts, big business, etc.) on a 1 to 5 scale: 1=Milquetoast, 2=Compromisers, 3=Moderately worked up, 4=Hardliners, and 5=Bombthrower. (These numbers represent Gifford's *opinion*, not hard facts.)

The column titled "Budget" includes total annual revenues and the percentage of those revenues used for the actual program (P).

The last and most infamous entry, Earth First! "defies charting," as one of its leaders told me over the telephone. Participants view themselves not as a *group* but as a *movement* of local greens ("up to 10,000") who gather for special events like 1990s "Redwood Summer" to act and "speak for the earth and trees." Their primary ongoing activity is publishing their newspaper, *Earth First!*

Group	Members	Purpose and Function	Budget	MB
1 National Wildlife Federation	5.8 mil	Promote wise use of resources through research, education, and publication	$90 mil P:68%	1
2 Greenpeace USA	1.8 mil	Fight global abuses, especially the slaughter of endangered sea mammals	$50 mil P:73%	4
3 World Wildlife Fund	1 mil	Preserve endangered wildlife and wildlands, especially in tropical forests	$32 mil P:85%	2
4 Sierra Club	644,231	Explore and preserve wilderness, inform public, influence political decisions	$40.6 mil P:74%	3
5 National Aududon Society	600,000	Protect wildlife, restore habitats, lobby, produce educational material	$37 mil P:73%	2
6 The Nature Conservancy	568,000	Protect land, preserve biodiversity. Manages over 1200 nature sanctuaries	$168.5 mil P:80.3%	1
7 Ducks Unlimited	519,000	Conserve and enhance North American wetland ecosystems	$67 mil P:76.3%	1
8 The Wilderness Society	400,000	Protect wildlands, wildlife, public lands and forests, Arctic refuge	$17.6 mil P:72%	3
9 Environmental Defense Fund	225,000	Link science, economics, and law to create economically viable solutions	$16.9 mil P:82%	3
10 Sierra Club Legal Defense Fund	180,000	Free legal services to other groups to enforce obedience to environmental laws	$8.2 mil P:76%	4
11 Natural Resources Defense Council	170,000	Monitor governmental agencies, inform, expose problems, litigate violations	$16 mil P:74%	4

12 African Wild-life Founda-tion	100,000	Support African conserva-tion through manage-ment-training, educa-tion, etc.	$4.6 mil P:83%	4
13 National Toxics Campaign	100,000	Network of 1,500 com-munity groups that moni-tor and lobby against toxic hazards	$1.5 mil P:86%	4
14 Defenders of Wildlife	80,000	Protect, restore wildlife communities e.g. Ever-glades, wolf reintro-duction	$4.3 mil P:64%	3
15 Friends of the Earth	50,000	Alert the public, lobby for action on ozone depletion, toxic chemicals, etc.	$3.1 mil P:81%	4
16 Earth Island Institute	35,000	Preserve and restore global environment. Focus: marine mammals, forests, urban habitats	$1.3 mil P:79%	4
17 Rainforest Action Network	35,000	Protect tropical rain-forests and the human rights of their inhabitants	$876,000 P:75%	4
18 League of Conservation Voters	30,000	Political arm of green groups. Monitors voting, endorses environ-mental candidates	$1.2 mil P:70%	3
19 Conservation International	24,000	Develop and implement ecosystem conservation projects, especially in rainforests	$10 mil P:85.5%	3
20 Environmental Action	20,000	Exposes problems and lobbies for strong laws. Works with local action groups on energy issues, toxics, and solid waste	$1.2 mil P:80%	4

21 Sea Shepherd Conservation Society	20,000	Direction action ocean patrol guarding marine mammals against illegal slaughter	$498,650 P:88%	5
22 Citizens Clearinghouse for Hazardous Waste	20,000	Equip local groups (over 7,300) with information and technical assistance to fight for environmental justice	$750,000 P:79%	5
23 American Rivers	17,000	Protect rivers and their environments from pollution and harmful development	$1.8 mil P:76%	3
24 Rainforest Alliance	15,000	Develop alternatives to deforestation: utilize forests without destroying them	$900,000 P:80%	2
25 Earth First!		Non-membership *movement* opposing human intrusion into nature	$80,000 P:92%	5

ADDRESSES AND RESOURCES

AFRICAN WILDLIFE FOUNDATION: 1717 Massachusetts Ave. NW, Washington, DC 29936. Membership is by donation. A $15 donation gains a subscription to quarterly newsletter, *Wildlife News.*

AMERICAN RIVERS: 801 Pennsylvania Ave. Suite 303, Washington, DC 20003. Membership ($20 per year) includes quarterly newsletter *American Rivers.*

CITIZENS CLEARINGHOUSE FOR HAZARDOUS WASTES: PO Box 926, Arlington, VA 22216. Membership ($25 per year) includes bimonthly magazine *Everyone's Backyard.*

CONSERVATION INTERNATIONAL: 1015 18th St. NW, Suite 1000, Washington, DC 20036.

DEFENDERS OF WILDLIFE: 1244 19th St. NW, Washington, DC 20036. Membership ($20 per year) includes bimonthly magazine *Defenders.*

DUCKS UNLIMITED: One Waterfowl Way, Long Grove, IL 60647. Monthly magazine *Ducks Unlimited* comes with $20 membership.

EARTH FIRST!: P.O. Box 5176, Missoula, MT 59068. (406) 728-8114. The *Earth First! Journal* is available for $20 per year.

EARTH ISLAND INSTITUTE: 300 Broadway, Suite 28, San Francisco, CA 94133. Membership ($25 per year) includes quarterly *Earth Island Journal.*

ENVIRONMENTAL ACTION: 1525 New Hampshire Ave. NW, Washington, DC 20036. Membership ($20 per year) includes bimonthly *Environmental Action Magazine.*

ENVIRONMENTAL DEFENSE FUND: 257 Park Avenue S., New York, NY 10010. Membership ($20 per year) includes quarterly *EDF Newsletter.*

FRIENDS OF THE EARTH: 218 D St. SE, Washington, DC 20003. Membership ($25 regular, $15 student/low income/senior citizen) includes monthly magazine *Not Man Apart.*

GREENPEACE USA: 1436 U St. NW, Washington, DC 20009. Membership ($20 per year) includes bimonthly *Greenpeace* magazine.

LEAGUE OF CONSERVATION VOTERS: 1150 Connecticut Ave. NW, Suite 201, Washington, DC 20036. Membership ($25 per year) includes *The National Environmental Scorecard.*

NATIONAL AUDUBON SOCIETY: 950 Third Ave., New York, NY 10022. Membership ($30 per year) includes bimonthly *Audubon Magazine*. An ornithological journal, *American Birds* is also available.

NATIONAL TOXIC CAMPAIGN: 1168 Commonwealth Ave., Boston, MA 02134. Membership ($25) includes quarterly *Toxic Times*.

NATIONAL WILDLIFE FEDERATION: 1400 16th St. NW, Washington, DC 20036. Monthly maazines *National Wildlife* and *International Wildlife* cost $15 each per year. *Ranger Rick*, a monthly magazine for children 6 to 12 years old, costs $14 per year. *Your Big Backyard*, a monthly magazine for 3 to 5 year-olds, costs $10.

NATIONAL RESOURCES DEFENSE COUNCIL: 40 W. 20th St., New York, NY 10011. Membership ($10) includes quarterly *The Amicus Journal* and bimonthly newsletter *Natural Resources Defense Council Newsline*.

THE NATURE CONSERVANCY: 1815 N. Lynn St., Arlington, VA 22209. Membership ($15) includes bimonthly *The Nature Conservancy Magazine* as well as state newsletters.

RAINFOREST ACTION NETWORK: 301 Broadway, Suite A, San Francisco, CA 94133. Membership ($25 regular, $15 limited income) includes monthly newsletter *Rain Forest Action Alert* and quarterly *World Rain Forest Report*.

RAINFOREST ALLIANCE: 270 Lafayette, #512, New York, NY 10012. Membership ($20 regular, $15 students and senior citizens) include quarterly newsletter *Canopy*.

SEA SHEPHERD CONSERVATION: P.O. Box 7000-S, Redondo Beach, CA 90277. Membership (by donation) includes quarterly newsletter *Sea Shepherd Log*.

SIERRA CLUB: 730 Polk St., San Francisco, CA 94109. Membership ($33 per year) includes subscription to monthly magazine *Sierra* and chapter publications.

SIERRA CLUB LEGAL DEFENSE FUND: 2044 Fillmore St., San Francisco, CA 94115.

THE WILDERNESS SOCIETY: 900 17th St., Washington, DC 20006. Membership ($15 first year, $30 subsequent years) includes bimonthly newsletter *The Wildlifer.*

WORLD WILDLIFE FUND: 1250 24th St. NW, Washington, DC 20037. Membership ($15 first year) includes bimonthly newsletter *Focus.*

Some of the above organizations have joined together in an effort to deal with population growth. National Wildlife Federation, the National Audubon Society, the Sierra Club, and the National Resources Defense Council are working together with Zero Population Growth and Planned Parenthood to lobby, educate, and advocate increased access to family planning for people around the world. Although Planned Parenthood promotes abortion, the above environmental groups indicated (in telephone conversations) an understandable reluctance to take an official position on the methods of family planning.

I only know of one organization that consistently maintains a biblical perspective on environmental issues:

Christian Nature Federation, P.O. Box 33000, Fullerton, CA 92633, (714) 447-9673. Membership ($25 per year) includes quarterly publication *Earthkeeper's Journal.*

Glossary

ACID RAIN: Rain formed when water vapor blends with toxic gases such as (1) sulphur and nitrogen oxides from power plants emissions or (2) huge quantities of sulfur dioxide spewed into the atmosphere by volcanic eruptions.

ATMOSPHERE: The layers of gases surrounding the earth.

AQUIFER: Groundwater, a rocky underground layer containing water.

BIODEGRADABLE: Can be broken down and converted to nutrients by the action of bacteria and other natural *decomposers.*

BIODIVERSITY: The rich diversity of living species on earth.

BIOSPHERE: The global *ecosystem* which includes the earth's landmass, waters, atmosphere, and living organisms.

COMPOSTING: Turning organic wastes into nutrient-rich soil.

DECOMPOSERS: Beetles, termites, worms, and other organisms that eat decaying matter and break it down into usable nutrients for plants.

DEFORESTATION: The total clearing of a forest.

DESERTIFICATION: The process by which productive (but usually marginal) land turns into desert.

EARTH-CENTERED SPIRITUALITY: The pagan belief that a universal life-force (spirit of Gaia, Mother Earth, Source, etc.) flows through every part of nature connecting everyone and everything. Through mental and spiritual formulas, human minds can connect with this force, manipulate its power and communicate its wisdom.

ECOLOGY: The science that studies how living species interact with each other and with their environments.

ECOSYSTEM: A community of organisms that interact with each other within a *habitat*.

FOOD CHAIN: A pyramid of interacting organisms that feed on each other from top (humans and large animals) to bottom (simple plants like plankton).

FOOD WEB: All the *food chains* within an *ecosystem*.

FOSSIL FUELS: Combustible oil, coal, natural gas, and other natural substances created deep within the earth.

GAIA: (1) The name for the ancient Greek earth goddess, (2) a "scientific" hypothesis by Dr. James Lovelock, who views the earth as a living, self-directing organism, (3) Earth as a feminine, pantheistic lifeforce that embodies and nurtures all of nature.

GREENHOUSE EFFECT: "Greenhouse gases" such as carbon dioxide and methane (from termites, gassy animals, and garbage dumps) trap heat. Many believe this will unleash a chain reaction of calamities from rising temperatures, melting icecaps and rising seas to cataclysmic floods, salted *aquifers*, and killer typhoons.

HABITAT: A place where a community of plants and animals live.

LANDFILL: A huge lined hole where garbage is layered with dirt and pressed down by tractors. Since most oxygen is squeezed out, even its *biodegradable* papers and plastics seldom *decompose*.

MANDALA: (Hindu and other earth-centered religions): lit. *orb*, geometric diagram drawn to protect from evil, invoke spirits, cast spells, contact the dead.... Similar to Buddhist WHEEL OF LIFE and the magical symbols drawn inside a circle for use in witchcraft. (See *quartered circle* in chart 4)

MONISM: The belief that All is One.

MONOTHEISM: Belief in one God (primarily Judaism, Christianity, and Islam)

OLD-GROWTH FOREST: A mature forest with centuries-old trees.

OZONE "HOLE": A seasonal thinning of the ozone layer of the stratosphere which shields the earth against the sun's ultraviolet rays. Monitored since 1979, it has appeared over the Antarctic between August and November.

PAGANISM: Seeking wisdom and drawing power from created things and demonic beings rather than from the Creator Himself *(Romans 1:18-25)*. It began when people first sought guidance from stars, parts of the earth, and demonic spirits. Today it usually refers to witchcraft, Goddess-worship, or the broad range of *earth-based religions*.

PAN-EN-THEISM: The belief that the universe is both *in* and a *manifestation of* God (the goddess, lifeforce, or Matthew Fox's Cosmic Christ) This "divinity" is both *transcendent* (above) creation and *immanent* (ever-present) in creation.

PANTHEISM: The belief that the divine lifeforce (god, goddess, truth) flows through every part of the universe.

POLYSTYRENE: A plastic foam used as insulation, cups and food containers. It is made with chlorofluorocarbons (CFSs) and is not biodegradable.

RENEWABLE RESOURCES: Wind, water, sunshine, certain trees, and other resources that can be replaced or replenished by natural processes or human practices.

SHAMAN: A pagan priest or medicine man or woman who functions as a medium between the physical and spiritual worlds.

STRATOSPHERE: The section of atmosphere that contains the ozone layer.

SUSTAINABLE DEVELOPMENT: Economic development that meets current needs without depleting resources that will be needed by future generations.

SYNCRETISM: A belief that blends diverse philosophies, religions, and spiritual practices into a single, unifying belief system.

VIRGIN (pagan meaning): A Goddess (Athena, Artemis, etc.) who is sexually active but refuses to submit to any man—and functions as a model for today's growing number of feminist pagans.

WATERSHED: The region drained by a network of streams, lakes, and rivers.

WETLANDS: Marshes and other moist, low-lying areas that provide rich habitats for certain plants and animals.

How to Live Free
from Demonic Oppression

As the wave of paganism spreads across the Western world, it leaves broken, hurting lives in its wake. Only God can free those who yield to the social currents and are trapped by occult practices. Satan's timeless bait (untamed lifestyles, hypnotic meditations, spiritism, various forms of divination, witchcraft techniques, and other occult forms of empowerment . . .) have separated countless people from God's protection and left them vulnerable to spiritual and demonic oppression.

Only God can restore freedom, and He uses His followers to extend that freedom to those who are in bondage. Know and share these foundational truths:

1. RECOGNIZE THAT YOU ARE INVOLVED IN SPIRITU-AL WARFARE. "For our struggle is not against flesh and blood, but against the rulers, against the authorities, against the powers of this dark world, and against the spiritual forces of evil in the heavenly realms" *(Ephesians 6:12)*.

2. BE EQUIPPED WITH GOD'S PROTECTIVE ARMOR. "Therefore put on the full armor of God" *(Ephesians 6:13)*. Review the steps shown in chapter 2.

While the most vital part of the armor is filling your mind with *truth* about God, don't ever enter a battle without "the breastplate of righteousness." This "breastplate" will help you to trust God to reveal any sin that separates you from God, confessing known sin, and trusting Him to fill you with His perfect life.

The only offensive part (the other parts are defensive) is the "sword of the Spirit which is the Word of God." Memorize key Scriptures needed in battle.

3. UNDERSTAND THE WEAKENING POWER OF SIN.
Spiritual bondage always begins with a sin problem. When
we disobey God, we forfeit His protection. If we persist in
sin, we open the door to spiritual bondage.

"Do not let the sun go down while you are still angry,"
wrote Paul, "and do not give the devil a *foothold*" (*Ephesians
4:27*). In other words, don't let sin trap you into addictive
behaviors by giving demonic forces a "foothold" or a
"place" of operation. Study and apply Romans 1:24-32 and
6:11-16.

4. WIELD GOD'S WORD AGAINST DEMONIC STRONG-
HOLDS. When Satan gains a place of operation, only one
weapon can break his foothold: God's spiritual sword, His
Word spoken with His authority. "For though we live in
the world, we do not wage war as the world does. The
weapons we fight with are not the weapons of the world.
On the contrary, we have divine power to demolish strong-
holds. We demolish arguments and every pretension that
sets itself up against the knowledge of God"
(*2 Corinthians 10:3-5*).

Know, affirm, and *speak* God's mighty Word against spiritual deception and oppression. Study Hebrews 4:12 and
Luke 4:1-13. See how Christ won the battle, and follow His
example.

5. UNDERSTAND THE BASIS FOR YOUR AUTHORITY
AND POWER IN CHRIST. What Jesus promised Peter two
thousand years ago, He promises us today: "I will give you
the keys of the kingdom of heaven; whatever you bind on
earth [shall have been] bound in heaven, and whatever you
loose on earth [shall have been] loosed in heaven" (*Matthew
16:19*).

God gives you power to make the spiritual victories of
His Kingdom effective and triumphant in your own life and
the lives of others. When you trust and follow Him, you are
a living extension of His life on earth—wielding His authority over all hindrances to the very highest and best God
offers us. All that Jesus accomplished on the cross is available for our victory today, for Jesus gave us spiritual keys

that can translate heavenly realities into practical earthly victories—*so that He is glorified and His purpose fulfilled.*.

KNOW WHAT CHRIST HAS ALREADY ACCOMPLISHED in the spiritual realm, then apply those victories to human life today. Notice that your authority and power to bind and loose is strictly limited to what He has already bound and loosed at the cross—that which "shall have *been* bound (or loosed) in heaven." It is also limited to God's timing and purpose. (Study *Matthew 16:19-26* and *18:15-20*.)

See what Christ has already bound and loosed. These triumphs show us the vast extent of your practical authority today—the victories you can claim for yourself and extend to another *as God leads*. At the cross Jesus:

* *Put* Satan in submission under His feet *(Ephesians 1:20-23)*

* *Disarmed* Satan's rulers and authorities *(Colossians 2:15)*

* *Drove out* the ruler of this world *(John 12:31)*

* *Destroyed* him [Satan] who holds the power of death *(Hebrews 2:14)*

* *Bound* Satan, "the strong man" *(Matthew 12:29)* who now fights by deception. In reality, he has already lost the war. When we proclaim God's victory, Satan must flee.

On the cross, Jesus also bore our sicknesses and carried our pain, became the guilt offering for all our sins (past, present, and future), offered total forgiveness, freed us from our selfish sin nature, and released in us His Kingdom-life of peace, wholeness, and love *(Isaiah 53:4-5, 10; Romans 4:7, 6:3-7, 8:1; Ephesians 1)*.

As you have trusted in Christ's work on the cross to join you to Himself, trust Him now for daily victory. Count on His promises and make them effective and practical to yourself and others. He who calls you to fulfill *His* purpose, will Himself accomplish it.

6. To release someone from spiritual bondage, follow the above steps, then PRAY, BASING YOUR PRAYER ON GOD'S WORD. For example:

Thank You, Lord, for the victory You won at the cross. You disarmed Satan and put him in submission under Your feet. In the name of Jesus Christ, I consider him bound and

banned from the life of _____. He has no place in
_____, no right to _____, who belongs to
You and is covered by Your blood. In Your name, I release
Your peace and strength into_____, so that
_____, might stand firm and immovable in You.
We praise You for *Your* victory, sovereign Lord and King.

Endnotes

CHAPTER 1

1. Richard N. Ostling, "When God Was a Woman," *Time* (6 May 1991): 73.
2. Elinor W. Gadon, *The Once and Future Goddess* (San Francisco: Harper & Row, 1989), 229–30.
3. Donald Bloesch, "Lost in the Mythical Myths," *Christianity Today* (19 August 1991): 23.
4. *Spaceship Earth: Our Global Environment*, a project of *The American Forum for Global Education* (45 John Street, Suite 1200, New York, N.Y. 10038). Contributors include Turner Broadcasting System, Ted Turner's Better World Society, Gaia Corporation, Tree People, National Wildlife Federation.
5. Thomas Berry, *The Dream of the Earth* (San Francisco: Sierra Club Books, 1988), 201.
6. Ibid., 87.
7. Julie Lanham, "The Greening of Ted Turner," *The Humanist* (November/December 1989): 6.
8. Barbara G. Walker, *The Woman's Encyclopedia of Myths and Secrets* (San Francisco: Harper & Row, 1983), 450.
9. Henry Morris, Ph.D., *The Biblical Basis for Modern Science* (Grand Rapids: Baker Book House, 1984), 37.
10. This attitude permeates environmental philosophies and literature. Much historical distortion was fomented through an article by Lynn White, Jr. titled, "The Historical Roots of Our Ecologic Crisis," *Science* (10 March 1967).
11. Elliot Miller, *A Crash Course on the New Age Movement* (Grand Rapids: Baker Book House, 1989), 87.
12. Matthew Fox, "What is *Creation?*" *Creation* (March/April 1990): 4.
13. Ibid., 18.
14. Michael and Alison Dowd, "A Christian Relationship to Earth," *Firmament* (Spring 1990): 3.

CHAPTER 2

1. Barry McWaters, *Conscious Evolution*, 10. Cited in Elliot Miller, *A Crash Course on the New Age Movement* (Grand Rapids; Baker Book House, 1989), 73.

2. Mike Samuels, M.D. and Hal Zina Bennett, *Well Body, Well Earth* (San Francisco: Sierra Club Books, 1983), 73.

3. As told by a participating parent in Walnut Creek, California.

4. Brooks Alexander, "Mind Power and the Mind's Eye," *SCP Journal* (Vol. 9:3, 1990): 14.

5. Thomas Berry, *The Dream of the Earth* (San Francisco: Sierra Club Books, 1988), 48.

6. Samuels and Bennett, 68.

7. Ibid., 69.

8. Ibid., 73.

9. Ephesians 6:12-18; Luke 8:30-36; 2 Corinthians 10:3-5; Zechariah 4:6.

10. Andy LePage, *Transforming Education* (Oakland, Calif.: Oakmore Press, 1987), back cover.

11. Ibid., 5.

12. Ibid., 17, 56, 118.

13. Ibid., back cover.

14. Suzanne Alexander, "Schools Sow Environmental Seeds Early," *The Wall Street Journal*, 26 June 1990.

15. Mike Weilbacher, "Education that Cannot Wait," *E Magazine* (March/April 1991): 30.

16. Ibid., 33.

17. Steve Van Matre, "Earth Spirit," *The Earth Speaks* (Warrenville, Ill.: The Institute for Earth Education, 1983), 125.

18. Ibid., 129.

19. "Parents Rally, Pull Kids from Class," *San Jose Mercury News*, 25 March 1991.

20. Brochure from Timperline Press Inc., Eugene, Ore. Jill Anderson developed the curriculum with the help of a government grant.

21. Bob Simonds, "President's Special Report—News Alert," May 1990 (Box 3200, Costa Mesa, Calif. 92628).

22. Mission S.O.A.R. Curriculum, 36. Cited by Bob Simonds.

23. C.S. Lewis, *Screwtape Letters* (New York: Bantam Books, 1982), xiii.

24. Joseph Cornell, *Sharing Nature with Children* (Nevada City, Calif.: Dawn Publications, 1979), 11–14.

25. Ibid., 6.

26. Joseph Cornell, *Listening to Nature* (Nevada City, Calif.: Dawn Publications, 1987), 68.

CHAPTER 3

1. Bill Devall and George Session, *Deep Ecology* (Salt Lake City: Gibbs Smith Publisher, 1985), ix.

2. Joseph Campbell, *The Power of Myth* (New York: Doubleday, 1988), 207.

3. Ibid., 22, 24.

4. *The New Lexicon Webster's Dictionary* (New York: Lexicon Publications, Inc., 1989), 660.

5. Deuteronomy 32:17; 1 Corinthians 10:20; Revelation 9:20.

6. Thomas Berry, *The Dream of the Earth* (San Francisco: Sierra Club Books, 1988), 34.

7. Ibid., 124.

8. Ibid., 41.

9. Paul Vitz, *Censorship—Evidence of Bias in Our Children's Textbooks* (Ann Arbor, Mich.: Servant Books, 1986) 3.

10. *Scholastic News*, Ed. 4, Vol. 53 (2 November 1990), 7. Statistics from Subscription Department, N.Y. (212) 505-3000.

11. Mary Micallef, *Floods & Droughts* (Carthage, Ill.: Good Apple, Inc., 1985), 7.

12. Jan Thurman-Veith, *Natural Wonders* (Palo Alto, Calif.: Monday Morning Books, 1986), 44.

13. Elaine Kitteredge, *Twelve* (Chicago: Optext, 1983), 4.

14. Ibid., 45.

15. Ibid., 12–13.

16. Michael A. Banks, *Understanding Science Fiction* (Morristown, N.J.: Silver Burdett Company, 1982), 11.

17. Ibid., 6.

18. Richard B. Bliss, Ed.D., *Good Science for Home and Christian Schools*, 4–6th grade (El Cajon, Calif.: Creation-Life Publishers, 1989), xv. (Minor change made with Dr. Bliss' permission).

19. Henry Morris, Ph.D., *The Genesis Record* (San Diego: Creation-Life Publishers, 1976), 74.

20. Tim Stafford, "Animal Lib," *Christianity Today* (18 June 1990): 19.

21. Ibid.

22. Dean A. Ohlman, "Confession Good for the Soul—and the Land," *Christian Nature Federation* (1 May 1991): 2.

23. Clark Wissler, Ph.D., *Indians* (New York: Anchor Books, Doubleday), 270.

24. Ibid., 8.

25. Ibid., 287.

26. Ibid., 63, 181.

27. Ibid., 131–32.

28. Ibid., 145.

CHAPTER 4

1. Starhawk, *Spiral Dance* (San Francisco: Harper & Row, 1979), 25.
2. Joseph Campbell, *The Power of Myth* (New York: Doubleday, 1988), 167.
3. Ari L. Goldman, "Religion Notes," *The New York Times*, 1 January 1991.
4. Starhawk, 16–17.
5. Judith Plant, *Healing the Wounds* (Santa Cruz: New Society Publishers, 1989), 216.
6. "Hard Copy," Fox (television), 20 July 1990.
7. Brochure for Bay Area Pagan Assemblies.
8. Kathleen B. Paquette, "Doorways into Women's Ritual: A Curriculum," 19 November 1987.
9. As told by another member of the class.
10. Phyllis Evelyn Johnson, "Which Step Are You On?" *Changes* (May–June 1990): 32.
11. Jeanie Geis Oliver, "Reading Selections for the Young Pagan," *Sage Woman* (Fall–Winter 9989 [1989]): 47.
12. Starhawk, 34, 91, 117, 208, 41, 186–87, 44, 42, 179, 199.
13. Susan Cooper, *The Dark Is Rising* (New York: Atheneum, 1982), 142, 122, 126, 75, 124, 161, 13, 108.
14. Starhawk, 123.
15. Ibid., 124.
16. Craig S. Hawkins, "The Modern World of Witchcraft," Part Two, *Christian Research Journal* (Summer 1990): 25. Hawkins quotes Starhawk, 11–12, 14.
17. Ibid., 24.

CHAPTER 5

1. Judith Weinraub, "The New Theology—Sheology, *The Washington Post*, 28 April 1991.
2. Sonia L. Nazario, "Is Goddess Worship Finally Going to Put Men in Their Place?" *The Wall Street Journal*, 7 June 1990.
3. Genesis 15:13-16.
4. Jennifer Barker Woolger and Roger J. Woolger, "The Wounded Goddesses Within," *New Realities* (March/April 1990): 11.
5. Ynestra King, "The Ecology of Feminism and the Feminism of Ecology," *Healing the Wounds* (Santa Cruz, Calif.: New Society Publishers, 1989), 19.
6. Carol P. Christ, "Why Women Need the Goddess: Phenomenological, Psychological, and Political Reflections," *Heresies* (Spring 1978): 277.

7. Elizabeth Roberts, *Dharma Gaia* (Berkeley: Parallax Press, 1990), 153.

8. "Invoking Ancient Gods for Modern Studies," *The New York Times*, 19 December 1990.

9. Ibid.

10. Weinraub.

11. Peterson's Guide to *Four Year Colleges 1991* (Princeton, NJ: Peterson's guides, 1991), 254.

12. Jacynth Hope-Simpson, *Cavalcade of Witches* (New York: H.Z. Walck, 1967) and Mildred Boyd, *Man, Myth, and Magic* (New York: Criterion Books, 1969).

13. Steven Erlanger, "Women Challenge Church Council Assembly," *The New York Times*, 2 February 1991.

14. Ellen Dahnke, "Athena Home at Last," *The Tennessean*, 21 May 1990.

15. Christine R. Downing, "The Mother Goddess among the Greeks," *The Book of the Goddess Past and Present* (New York: The Crossroad Publishing Company, 1989), 49.

16. Peter Steinfels, "Idyllic Theory of Goddesses Creates Storm," *The New York Times*, 13 February 1990.

17. Ibid.

18. Ibid.

19. Ibid.

20. Judith Plant, *Healing the Wounds* (Santa Cruz: New Society Publishers, 1989), 3.

21. Barbara G. Walker, *The Woman's Encyclopedia of Myths and Secrets* (San Fransisco: Harper & Row, 1983), 346.

22. Ibid., 263.

23. Ibid., 264.

24. Joseph Campbell, *The Power of Myth* (New York: Doubleday, 1988), 99.

25. *Encyclopaedia Britannica* XII (Chicago: William Benton), 661.

26. Elinor Gadon, *The Once and Future Goddess* (San Francisco: Harper & Row, 1989), 115.

27. Carl Olsen, *The Book of the Goddess Past and Present* (New York: Crossroad, 1989), 1.

28. Otto Baab, *The Theology of the Old Testament* (New York: Abingdon-Cokesbury, 1949), 105, 110. Cited by Paul C. Vitz, *Psychology As Religion* (Grand Rapids: William B. Eerdmans Publishing Co., 1988), 93.

29. Henry Morris, *The Genesis Record* (San Diego: Creation-Life Publishers, 1976), 264.

30. Walker, 451.

31. Ibid., 452.

CHAPTER 6

1. Joanna Macy, "The Greening of the Self," *Dharma Gaia*, (Berkeley:

Parallax Press, 1990), 53.

2. Mike Wyatt, "Humanism and Ecology: the Social Ecology/Deep Ecology Schism," *Green Synthesis* (October 1989): 8.

3. Elizabeth Koda-Callan, *The Magic Locket* (New York: Workman Publishing, 1988), 12.

4. Ibid., 30.

5. Virginia Satir, *Meditations and Inspirations* (Berkeley: Celestial Arts, 1985), 15, 26, 29.

6. Calvin Miller, *The Finale* (Downers Grove, Ill.: InterVarsity Press, 1979), 29–30.

7. Ibid., 60, 70–71.

8. Marion Woodman, *The Pregnant Virgin* (Toronto: Inner City Books, 1985), back cover.

9. Jennifer Barker Woolger and Roger J. Woolger, "The Wounded Goddesses Within," *New Realities* (March/April 1990): 11.

10. Ibid., 13.

11. Carl Jung, *Man and His Symbols* (New Haven: Yale University Press, 1938), 95.

12. Elinor W. Gadon, *The Once and Future Goddess* (San Francisco: Harper & Row, 1989), 230.

13. Brooks Alexander, "Mind Power and the Mind's Eye," *SCP Journal* (Vol. 9:3, 1990): 15.

14. Doug Groothuis, *Revealing the New Age Jesus* (Downers Grove, Ill.: InterVarsity Press, 1990), 76.

15. Satir, 23.

16. Ibid.

17. Virginia Satir, *Self Esteem* (Milbrae, Calif.: Celestial Arts, 1970), 41–42.

18. Alexander, 9.

19. Paul C. Vitz, *Psychology As Religion* (Grand Rapids: Eerdmans Publishing Company, 1977), 93.

20. *The Family Educator*, "Who Would Build on a Crumbled Foundation" (March/April 1990): 3.

21. Cassette tapes of Dr. Coulson's messages can be ordered from the Research Council on Ethnopsychology, 2054 Oriole Street, San Diego, CA 92114.

22. Ibid.

23. John Bradshaw, *The Family* (Deerfield Beach, Fla.: Health Communications, Inc., 1988), 229.

24. Ibid.

25. Charles Colson, *Against the Night* (Ann Arbor, Mich.: Servant Publications, 1989), 98.

26. Ibid.

27. Ibid.

28. Oswald Chambers, *My Utmost for His Highest* (New York: Dodd, Mead & Company, 1935), 279.

29. Ibid., 246.

30. Benjamin Schmolck, 1672–1737.

CHAPTER 7

1. Elinor W. Gadon, *The Once and Future Goddess* (San Francisco: Harper & Row, 1989), xv.

2. Brian Swimme, *The Universe Is a Green Dragon* (Santa Fe, N.M.: Bear & Company, Inc., 1984), 49.

3. United Press International, "New Study of Teenage Sex," *San Francisco Chronicle*, 5 January 1991.

4. Don Feder, "Colleges Facilitate Intramural Sex," *AFA Journal* (November/December 1990): 23.

5. Richard Harrington, "Madonna Thriving On Her Own Chaos," *San Francisco Chronicle*, 5 December 1990.

6. Ibid.

7. Camille Paglia, "Madonna—Finally, a Real Feminist," *The New York Times*, December 14, 1990.

8. Jay Cocks, "Madonna Draws the Line," *Time* (17 December 1990): 74.

9. Tom Sabulis, "Her Fans Speak Out on Spanking," *San Jose Mercury News*, 20 May 1990.

10. Cocks, 74.

11. Ibid., 75.

12. Harry Sumrall, "Madonna's Tour Spotlights Her Ego More Than Her Talent," *San Jose Mercury News*, 20 May 1990.

13. Matthew Fox, "My Final Statement Before Being Silenced By the Vatican," *Earth Island Journal* (Winter 1988–89): 50.

14. Carol P. Christ, *Laughter of Aphrodite* (San Francisco: Harper & Row, 1987), 176–77.

15. Ibid., 188.

16. *The Encyclopaedia Britannica, Vol. 2* (Chicago: Encyclopaedia Brittanica, Inc., 1968), 110–111.

17. Judy Harrow, "A Season with Aphrodite," *Gnosis* (Fall 1990): 17.

18. Joseph Campbell, *The Power of Myth* (New York: Doubleday, 1988), 182.

19. Peter L. Berger, "Cakes for the Queen of Heaven: 2500 Years of Religious Ecstasy," *The Christian Century* (December 25, 1974): 1218–1219.

20. Andy LePage, Ph.D., *Transforming Education* (Oakland, Calif.: Oakmore House Press, 1987), 118.

21. Pupul Jayakar, *Earth Mother* (San Francisco: Harper & Row, 1990), 134.

22. Tal Brooke, "Myths—Adhesive for a Generic Religion," *SCP Journal* (Vol. 9:2, 1990): 8–9.

23. Alice Walker, *The Color Purple* (New York: Washington Square Press, 1982), 187.

24. David Hinckley, " 'Dick Tracy' Shouldn't Have Sex,' *The San Jose Mercury News,* 25 June 1990.

25. Berger, 1219.

26. W.F. Albright, *From the Stone Age to Christianity,* 214. Cited by Merrill F. Unger, *Archeology and the Old Testament* (Grand Rapids, Mich.: Zondervan, 1977), 177.

27. James B. Pritchard, editor, *Ancient Near Eastern Texts* (Princeton, N.J.: Princeton University Press, 1969), 394.

CHAPTER 8

1. Brian Tokar, *The Green Alternative* (San Pedro, Calif.: R. & E. Miles, 1987), 150.

2. Chevron advertisement, *Time* (12 February 1990).

3. Joseph Campbell, *The Power of Myth* (New York: Doubleday, 1988), 207.

4. Ibid., 99.

5. "Puppets for Social Change," *San Francisco Chronicle,* 3 March 1991.

6. Michael Brenson, "African and Other Portraits, Side by Side," *The New York Times,* 3 August 1990.

7. Adriana Diaz, "The Earth's Alive! Festival," *Creation* (May/June 1990): 35.

8. "Arts and Culture," *Green Letter* (Summer 1990): 51–52.

9. Francis Schaeffer, *How Then Shall We Live?* (Old Tappan, N.J.: Fleming H. Revell Company, 1976), 124.

10. Ibid., 159.

11. Os Guiness, *The Dust of Death* (Downers Grove, Ill.: InterVarsity Press, 1973), 234.

12. Ibid., 325.

13. Francis Schaeffer, *Escape from Reason* (Downers Grove, Ill.: InterVarsity Press, 1968), 56.

14. Ibid., 55.

15. Bill Devall and George Session, *Deep Ecology* (Salt Lake City: Peregrine Smith Books, 1985), 74.

16. Ibid., 84.

17. Galen Rowell, "The Dalai Lama's Tibet, *San Jose Mercury News,* 9 December 1990.

18. Andy LePage, *Transforming Education* (Oakland, Calif.: Oakmore House Press, 1987), 129.

19. Matthew Fox, "Mysticism: The Universal Experience," *Creation* (September/October 1988): 11.

20. James F. Cooper, "Art Censors: A Closer Look at the NEA," *New Dimensions* (June 1991): 26.

21. Ibid., 28.

22. Ibid., 28.

23. H.R. Rookmaker, *Art Needs No Justification* (Downers Grove, Ill.: InterVarsity Press, 1978), 45.

24. G V editores, *National Museum of Anthropology Mexico* (Mexico City: Grupo Cultural Especializado, 1990), 54.

25. Clark Wissler, *Indians of the United States* (New York: Doubleday, 1966), 155.

26. Information gathered from the various volumes of *Encyclopedia of World Art* (note #25) and *Encyclopedia Brittanica;* from the National Museum of Anthropology Mexico; from Bill Musk's *The Unseen Face of Islam,* (Eastbourne, Great Britain: MARC, 1989); and with helpful counsel from Brooks Alexander, founder of Spiritual Counterfeits Project.

27. Brooks Alexander, *SCP Journal* (Vol 9:3, 1990): 9.

28. Ibid., 10.

CHAPTER 9

1. The Dalai Lama, *My Tibet* (Berkeley: University of California Press, 1990), 81.

2. Bill Devall and George Session, *Deep Ecology* (Salt Lake City: Gibbs Smith Publisher, 1985), 206.

3. Peter Russell, *The Global Brain* (Los Angeles: J.P. Tarcher, Inc., 1983), 164.

4. Susan Hooper, "Educator Proposes a Global 'Core Curriculum,'" *Education Week* (27 November 1985): 8. Cited by Eric Buehrer, *The New Age Masquerade* (Brentwood, Tenn.: Wolgemuth & Hyatt, Publishers, Inc., 1990), 74.

5. Robert Muller, *New Genesis: Shaping a Global Spirituality* (Garden City, N.Y.: Doubleday and Co., 1848), 145.

6. Ibid., 153.

7. Eric Buehrer, *The New Age Masquerade* (Brentwood, Tenn.: Wolgemuth & Hyatt, Publishers, Inc., 1990), 117.

8. *Encyclopaedia Britannica*, Vol. 15 (Chicago: Encyclopaedia Britannica, Inc., 1968), 640.

9. Dr. Anis A. Shorrosh, *Islam Revealed* (Nashville: Thomas Nelson Publishers, 1988). Also told by Ron Carlson in lecture titled *Islam.* Audio cassette from Christian Ministries International (7601 Superior Terrace, Eden Prairie Minn.).

10. J. Dudley Woodberry, "The March of Islam Across the Centuries," *Target Earth* (Pasadena, Calif.: Global Mapping International, 1989), 124.

11. *Wrestling with Dark Angels,* eds. C. Peter Wagner and F. Douglas Pennoyer (Ventura, Calif.: Regal Books, 1990), 317.

12. Bill Musk's *The Unseen Face of Islam* (Eastbourne, Great Britain: MARC, 1989), 223.

13. *Encyclopaedia Britannica,* Vol. 20 (Chicago: Encyclopaedia Britannica, Inc., 1968), 695.

14. 1 John 4:1; Matthew 7:16 (NASB); 1 Thessalonians 5:21.

15. Marilyn Ferguson, *The Aquarian Conspiracy* (Los Angeles: J.P. Tarcher, Inc., 1976), 369.

16. Buehrer, 114.

17. Philip Vander Velde and Hyung-Chan Kim, eds., *Global Mandate: Pedagogy for Peace* (Bellingham, Wash.: Bellwether Press, 1985), 10. Cited by Buehrer, 114.

18. "Government Tells Churches What to Teach," *AFA Journal* (October 1989): xx.

19. "Hate Literature Laws Sweep the U.S. and Other Western Democracies," *The Christian World Report* (April, 1989): 1.

20. Gary L. Bauer, "Colleges: Watch Out for the Sensitivity Police," *Washington Watch* (December 1990): 4.

21. "Is the U.S. on the Verge of Criminalizing Christianity?" *The Christian World Report,* (November 1989): 1.

22. Matthew 28:19.

23. Lewis M. Simons, "Me-First Cults Thrive in Japan," *San Jose Mercury News,* April 16, 1990.

24. Don Lattin, "Esalen Institute's Ties with Soviet Philosophy Project," *San Francisco Chronicle,* 6 November 1990.

25. Rabi R. Maharaj, *East-West Gospel Ministries* Newsletter, December 1, 1990.

Index